DEEP FURROWS

*Which Tells of Pioneer Trails Along Which the Farmers of
Western Canada Fough Their Way to Great Achievements
in Co-Operation*

HOPKINS MOORHOUSE

1st WORLD
LIBRARY
Literary Society

Deep Furrows

Hopkins Moorhouse

© 1st World Library, 2007
PO Box 2211
Fairfield, IA 52556
www.1stworldlibrary.com
First Edition

LCCN: 2007930796

Softcover ISBN: 978-1-4218-4840-2
Hardcover ISBN: 978-1-4218-4743-6
eBook ISBN: 978-1-4218-4937-9

Purchase *"Deep Furrows"*
as a traditional bound book at:
www.1stWorldLibrary.com/purchase.asp?ISBN=978-1-4218-4840-2

1st World Library is a literary, educational organization
dedicated to:

- Creating a free internet library of downloadable ebooks

- Hosting writing competitions and offering book publishing
  scholarships.

Interested in more 1st World Library books? contact:
literacy@1stworldlibrary.com
Check us out at: www.1stworldlibrary.com

1ˢᵗ World Library Literary Society

Giving Back to the World

"If you want to work on the core problem, it's early school literacy."

- James Barksdale, former CEO of Netscape

"No skill is more crucial to the future of a child, or to a democratic and prosperous society, than literacy."

- Los Angeles Times

"Literacy... means far more than learning how to read and write... The aim is to transmit... knowledge and promote social participation."

- UNESCO

"Literacy is not a luxury, it is a right and a responsibility. If our world is to meet the challenges of the twenty-first century we must harness the energy and creativity of all our citizens."

- President Bill Clinton

"Parents should be encouraged to read to their children, and teachers should be equipped with all available techniques for teaching literacy, so the varying needs and capacities of individual kids can be taken into account."

- Hugh Mackay

TO THE

MEN AND WOMEN OF THE SOIL

CONTENTS

.

FOREWORD

Once in awhile, maybe, twenty-five or thirty years ago, they used to pack you off during the holidays for a visit on Somebody's Farm. Have you forgotten? You went with your little round head close clipped till all the scar places showed white and you came back with a mat of sunbleached hair, your face and hands and legs brown as a nut.

Probably you treasure recollections of those boyhood days when a raw field turnip, peeled with a "toad-stabber," was mighty good eatin'. You remember the cows and chickens, the horses, pigs and sheep, the old corn-crib where generally you could scare up a chipmunk, the gnarled old orchard—the Eastern rail-fenced farm of a hundred-acres-or-so. You remember Wilson's Emporium at the Corners where you went for the mail—the place where the overalled legs of the whole community drummed idly against the cracker boxes and where dried prunes, acquired with due caution, furnished the juvenile substitute for a chew of tobacco!

Or perhaps you did not know even this much about country life—you of the Big Cities. To you, it may be, the Farmer has been little more than the caricatures of the theatres. You have seen him wearing blue jeans or a long linen duster in "The Old Homestead," wiping his eyes with a big red bandana from his hip pocket. You have seen him dance eccentric steps in wrinkled cowhide boots, his hands beneath flapping coat-tails, his chewing jaws constantly moving "the little bunch of spinach on his chin!" You have heard him fiddle away like two-sixty at "Pop Goes the Weasel!" You have grinned while he sang through his nose about the great big hat with the great big brim, "All Ba-ound Ra-ound With a Woolen String!"

Yes, and you used to read about the Farmer, too—Will Carleton's farm ballads and legends; Riley's fine verses about the frost on the pumpkin and "Little Orphant Annie" and "Over the Hill to the Poorhouse!" And when Cousin Letty took you to the Harvest Home Supper and Grand Entertainment in the Town Hall you may have heard the village choir wail: "Oh, *Shall* We Mortgage the Farm?"

Perhaps even yet, now that you are man grown—business or professional man of the great cities—perhaps even yet, although you long have studied the market reports and faithfully have read the papers every day—perhaps that first impression of what a farmer was like still lingers in a more or less modified way. So that to you pretty much of an "Old Hayseed" he remains. Thus, while you have been busy with other things, the New Farmer has come striding along until he has "arrived in our midst" and to you he is a stranger.

Remember the old shiny black mohair sofa and the wheezy, yellow-keyed melodeon or the little roller hand-organ that used to play "Old Hundred"? They have given place to new styles of furniture, upright pianos and cabinet gramophones. Coffin-handles and wax flowers are not framed in walnut and hung in the Farmer's front parlor any more; you will find the grotesque crayon portrait superseded by photo enlargements and the up-to-date kodak. The automobile has widened the circle of the Farmer's neighbors and friends, while the telephone has wiped distance from the map.

In the modern farm kitchen hot and cold water gushes from bright nickel taps into a clean white enamel sink, thanks to the pneumatic water supply system. The house and other farm buildings are lighted by electricity and perhaps the little farm power plant manages to operate some machinery—to drive the washing machine, the cream separator, the churn and the fodder-cutter or tanning-mill. There is also a little blacksmith shop and a carpenter shop where repairs can be attended to without delay. True, all these desirable conveniences may not be possessed generally as yet; but the Farmer has seen them working on the model farmstead exhibited by the Government at the Big Fair or in the Farm Mechanics car of the Better Farming Special Trains that have toured the country, and he dreams about them.

More scientific methods of agriculture have been adopted. The Farmer has learned what may be accomplished by crop rotations and new methods of cultivation. He has learned to analyze the soil and grow upon his land those crops for which it is best suited. If he keeps a dairy herd he tests each cow and knows exactly how her yield is progressing so that it is impossible for her to "beat her board bill." No longer is it even considered good form to chop the head off the old rooster; the Farmer sticks him scientifically, painlessly, instantaneously dressing him for market in the manner that commands the highest price. So with the butter, the eggs and all the rest of the farm products.

Do you wonder that the great evolution of farming methods should lead to advanced thought upon the issues of the day? In the living room the Family Bible remains in its old place of honor, perhaps with the crocheted mat still doing duty; but it is not now almost the only book in the house. There is likely to be a sectional bookcase, filled with solid volumes on all manner of practical and economic subjects—these as well as the best literature, the latest magazines and two or three current newspapers.

Yes, a whole flock of tin roosters have rusted away on top of the barn since the Farmer first began to consider himself the Rag Doll of Commerce and to seek adjustments. It is the privilege of rag dolls to survive a lot of abuse; long after wax has melted and sawdust run the faithful things are still on hand. And along about crop time the Farmer finds himself attracting a little attention.

That is because this business of backbone farming is the backbone of Business In General. As long as money is circulating freely Business In General, being merely an exchange in values, wears a clean shirt and the latest cravat. But let some foreign substance clog the trade channels and at once everything tightens up and squeezes everybody.

Day by day the great mass of the toilers in the cities go to work without attempting to understand the fluctuations of supply and demand. They are but cogs on the rim, dependent for their little revolutions upon the power which drives the machinery. That power being Money Value, any wastage must be replaced by the creation of new wealth. So men turn to the soil for salvation—to the greatest manufacturing concern in the world, Nature Unlimited. This is the plant of which the Farmer is General Manager.

On state occasions, therefore, it has been the custom in the past to call him "the backbone of his country"—its "bone and sinew." Without him, as it were, the Commercial Fabric could not sit up in its High Chair and eat its bread and milk. Such fine speeches have been applauded loudly in the cities, too frequently without due thought—without it occurring to anyone, apparently, that perhaps the Farmer might prefer to be looked upon rather as an ordinary hard-working human being, entitled as such to "a square deal."

But all these years times have been changing. Gradually Agriculture has been assuming its proper place in the scheme of things. It is recognized now that successful farming is a business—a profession, if you like—requiring lifelong study, foresight, common sense, close application; that it carries with it all the satisfaction of honest work well done, all the dignity of practical learning, all the comforts of modern invention, all the wider benefits of clean living and right thinking in God's sunny places.

And with his increasing self-respect the New Farmer is learning to command his rights, not merely to ask and accept what crumbs may fall. He is learning that these are the days of Organization, of Co-Operation among units for the benefit of the Whole; that by pooling his resources he is able to reach the Common Objective with the least waste of effort.

He has become a power in the land.

These pages record a story of the Western Canadian farmer's upward struggle with market conditions—a story of the organized Grain Growers. No attempt is made to set forth the full details of the whole Farmer's Movement in Western Canada in all its ramifications; for the space limits of a single volume do not permit a task so ambitious.

The writer has endeavored merely to gather an authentic record of the earlier activities of the Grain Growers' Associations in the three Prairie Provinces—why and how they came to be organized, with what the farmers had to contend and something of their remarkable achievements in co-operative marketing during the past decade. It is a tale of strife, limned by high lights and some shadows. It is a record worthy of preservation and one which otherwise would pass in some of its details with the fading memories of the pathfinders.

If from these pages the reader is able to glean something of interest, something to broaden—be it ever so slightly—his understanding of the Western Canadian farmers' past viewpoint and present outlook, the undertaking will have found its justification and the long journeys and many interviews their reward.

For, under the alchemy of the Great War, many things are changing and in the wonderful days of reconstruction that lie ahead the Farmer is destined to play an upstanding part in the new greatness of our country. Because of this it behooves the humblest citizen of us to seek better understanding, to meet half way the hand of fellowship which he extends for a new conception of national life.

The writer is grateful to those farmers, grain men, government officials and others who have assisted him so kindly in gathering and verifying his material. Indebtedness is acknowledged also to sundry Dominion Government records, to the researches of Herbert N. Casson and to the press and various Provincial Departments of Agriculture for the use of their files.

H.M.

WINNIPEG, March 1st, 1918.

CHAPTER I

THE MAN ON THE QU'APPELLE TRAIL

Among the lonely lakes I go no more,
For she who made their beauty is not there;
The paleface rears his tepee on the shore
And says the vale is fairest of the fair.
Full many years have vanished since, but still
The voyageurs beside the camp-fire tell
How, when the moon-rise tips the distant hill,
They hear strange voices through the silence swell.

—*E. Pauline Johnson.*
The Legend of Qu'Appelle.

To the rimming skyline, and beyond, the wheatlands of Assiniboia[1] spread endlessly in the sunshine. It was early October in the year 1901—one of those clear bright days which contribute enchantment to that season of spun gold when harvest bounties are garnered on the Canadian prairies. Everywhere was the gleam of new yellow stubble. In serried ranks the wheat stocks stretched, dwindling to mere specks, merging as they lost identity in distance. Here and there stripes of plowed land elongated, the rich black freshly turned earth in sharp contrast to the prevailing gold, while in a tremendous deep blue arch overhead an unclouded sky swept to cup the circumference of vision. Many miles away, yet amazingly distinct in the rarefied air, the smoke of threshers hung in funnelled smudges above the horizon—like the black smoke of steamers, hull down, at sea.

On this particular autumn afternoon a certain black dot might have been observed, so lost in the immensity of landscape that it appeared to be stationary. It was well out upon the trail that wound northward from Indian Head into the country of the Fishing Lakes—the trail that forked also eastward to dip through the valley of the Qu'Appelle at Blackwood before striking north and east across the Kenlis plain towards the Pheasant Hills. In reality the well kept team which drew the big grain wagon was swinging steadily ahead at a smart pace; for their load of supplies, the heaviest item of which was a new plow, was comparatively light, they were homeward bound and the going in the earlier stages of the long journey was smooth.

The driver sat hunched in his seat, reins sagging. He was a man of powerful physique, his skin deep coppered by long exposure to prairie winds and sun. In repose the face that was shadowed by the wide felt hat would have appeared somewhat deceptive in its placidity owing to the fact that the strong jaw and firm mouth were partly hidden by a heavy moustache and a thick, black beard, trimmed short.

Just now it was evident that the big farmer's mood was far from pleasant. Forearm on knee, he had surrendered completely to his thoughts. His fists clenched spasmodically and there was an angry glint in his eyes. Occasionally he shook his head as if the matter in mind were almost too hopeless for consideration. A sudden surge of resentment made him lash his booted leg with the ends of the lines.

"Confound them!" he muttered aloud.

Hopkins Moorhouse

He had just delivered his first load of the season's new wheat. Three nights before, by lantern light, he had backed his horses to the wagon and hauled it twenty-five miles to the railway at Indian Head. His stay there had not been conducive to peace of mind.

To reach the rails with a heavy load in favorable weather was simple enough; it merely required time. But many such trips would be necessary before his crop was marketed. Some of the farmers from beyond the Qu'Appelle would be hauling all winter; it was in winter that the haul was long and cruel. Starting at one, two or three o'clock in the morning, it would be impossible to forecast the weather with any degree of accuracy, so that often they would be overtaken by blizzards. At such times the lack of stopping-places and shelter in the sparsely settled reaches of the trail encompassed the journey with risks every whit as real as pioneer perils of marauding Indians or trailing wolf-packs.

Snow and wind, however, had no place in the thoughts of the lonely farmer at the moment. Such things he had been used to ever since he first homesteaded; this long haul with the products of his toil he had been making for many years. What immediately concerned him was the discouraging prospect of another wheat blockade instead of any improvement in conditions which had become unbearable. With the country as full of wheat as it was this year it required no great gift of prophecy to foretell what would happen.

It was happening already. The railway people were ignoring completely the car-distribution clauses of the Grain Act and thereby playing in with the elevator interests, so that the farmers were going to be just where they were before—at the mercy of the buyers, their legitimate profits filched by excessive dockage, low grades, depressed prices, exorbitant storage charges, even short weights in some cases. All this in spite of the strong agitation which had led to Government action, in spite of the Royal Commission which had investigated the farmers' claims and had recommended the Grain Act, in spite of the legislation on the statutes! Law or no law, the farmer was still to be preyed upon, apparently, without a single weapon left with which—

The eyes of the man in the broad-brimmed hat grew grave. Scoff as he might among the men of the district when the serious ones voiced their fears to him, his own thoughts always came back to those fears. From the Red River Valley to the foothills long-smouldering indignation was glowing like a streak of fire in the prairie grass; a spark or two more and nothing could stop the conflagration that would sweep the plains country. If the law were to fail these red-blooded and long-suffering homesteaders there would be final weapons alright—real weapons! It was no use shutting one's eyes to the danger. Some fool would do something rash, and with the farmers already inflamed and embittered, there was no telling what desperate things might be attempted.

That was the fear which stirred and perplexed the solitary traveller; for he had heard things that afternoon—seen things that he did not like but could not ignore. He recognized an undercurrent of feeling, a silence more ominous than all the heated talk, and that was where the danger lay. Something would have to be done, and that soon. But what? What?

So engrossed was he that beyond an occasional flip of the reins or a word to the horses he paid no heed to his surroundings. A huge jack-rabbit sprang up, almost from beneath the noses of the team, and went flying off in great leaps over the stubble. A covey of prairie chicken, fat and fit, whirred into the air and rocketed away. But he scarcely saw them. Had he looked up he might have noticed a horseman loping down a cross trail with the evident intention of heading off the wagon. But the rider had pounded almost within hailing distance before the other was aware of his approach.

It was Bob McNair of the "Two-Bar Ranch," as he insisted upon calling his wheat farm. He waved an oil-spattered Stetson and came into the trail with a rush, pulling up the wiry broncho with a suddenness that would have unseated one less accustomed than McNair, former corporal, Royal North-West Mounted Police.

"Howdy, W. R. Thought 'twas your outfit. Good job I aint a Blackfoot on the warpath," he laughed. "I'd sure 'a' had your scalp sneaked before you could draw a bead!" He swung alongside, stepped into the wagon, looped the bridle-rein over the handle of the new plow and, climbing forward, shook hands heartily and sat down.

"You're looking fit, Bob," welcomed the other with evident pleasure. "What brings you over this way? Everything going alright?"

"So-so," nodded McNair. "Been over Sintaluta to see about gettin' a car, among other things."

"Of course you got it?"

"Sure! Oh, sure I got it—got it still to get!" and McNair burst into a flow of language that did even him justice. More or less vehement at all times, the one-time corporal exhibited so much vigor in his remarks that his good-natured auditor had to laugh. "I ain't tryin' to be funny!" finished McNair. "I mean every dashed word of it, Motherwell. If I don't get some of it out o' my system I'll bust to bits, that's what. Say, I met Sibbold. He told me some of you fellows was meetin' over at the Head to-day. What about it?"

"Why, yes, Johnny Millar got a few of us together to talk things over. Lot of talk alright. Some of the boys were feeling pretty hot, I can tell you! But I can't see that anything came of it except some resolutions—the usual sort, you know."

"Pshaw! I was hopin' it meant action of some kind." The ex-rancher was silent for a moment. Then his right fist went into his left palm with a smack. "The only kind o' resolution that'll get anythin' is made o' lead and fits in a rifle breech! And I want to tell you, old man, if there ain't some pretty quick right-about-facin' in certain quarters, I'll be dashed if I ain't for it! An' I won't be standin' alone, either!" he added grimly.

W. R. Motherwell[2] glanced sharply at the tense face.

"Don't talk nonsense!" he reproved quietly.

"I ain't talkin' nonsense. Not on your life! If I am, then I reckon I know a hundred or so hard-headed farmers who're doin' the identical same. An' if I know that many in my territory, W. R., how many d'you suppose there are if we take in Manitoba and clean through to the mountains?"

"Then all I've got to say is: there are more and bigger fools in the country than I had any idea of."

"What d'you mean, talkin' like that?"

"That's just what I've got to say to you, McNair," retorted the big farmer with heat. "What do *you* mean, talking like that? If you're serious in what you say—"

"I said I was, didn't I?" snapped the other.

Hopkins Moorhouse

"Then you ought to be tied up on the Two-Bar and muzzled, for you're plumb mad, McNair! It's just that kind of firebrand talk that's hurting our cause. The farmers have got enough enemies now, God knows, without making a lot of new ones. Doggone your hide, Mac, what're you trying to do?—Stir up another rebellion like that of '85?"

"If it's necessary—you bet I am!" he brazened.

"You, of all men!"

"An' why not me? Just because I've worn the Queen's uniform, eh? Well, let me tell you, sir, I belonged to a body of men who stood for British justice an' a square deal to even the meanest Injun in the Territories." The ex-mounted policeman spoke with pride. "We'd never have handled the beggars if it hadn't been for that. Even the Injuns were men enough to recognize justice, an' that's more'n these commercial blood-suckers to-day can do! If our case was in the hands of the Force it'd rest on its merits an' us grain growers'd get justice. Instead, where is it?—in the hands of a pussy-footed, hifalutin' bunch o' political windbags in the East who don't care a damn about us hayseeds out West! An' what's more—"

"The Royal Mounted stood for law and order, Bob; but you'd class yourself with the half-breeds, would you? Have another little rebellion like that of '85 with all the—"

"Not like '85," interrupted the rancher. "No, sir, this one'll be bloodless; but it'll knock the spots off the 'breeds' little shindig all the samee!"

"You spoke of rifles, McNair. Guns go off," interpolated the other sententiously. "What'n the mischief do you expect to gain by that sort of thing?"

"A hearing, by Jingo! That's more'n all your letters to the papers an' your meetin's an' resolutions have got us. We'll show 'em we mean business—"

"Rot! How did we get the Royal Commission except by those letters and meetings? That put the Manitoba Grain Act on the statutes, didn't it? Mean to say we're no farther ahead? We've got the whole grain trade under control and supervision—"

"Like ducks you have!" The former rancher threw back his head and laughed.

"We've got the privilege of loading our wheat direct on cars through the flat warehouses or any other way we like—"

"What's the good o' that if a man can't get a car when he wants it?" demanded McNair impatiently. "The elevator gang 've organized to grab everything in sight. I know it. You know it. Everybody knows it, by heaven! So what's the use o' talkin'?"

"We've got to be fair, though. The elevator people have put a lot of money—Say, why can't we organize, too?" suggested Motherwell with a flash of inspiration. "We haven't tried that yet. That's constitutional. That's what the livestock breeders have done," he said eagerly.

McNair shook his head.

"I tell you, Bill, it's too late for that sort o' thing," he objected. "Unless you mean organizin' to fight—"

"Exactly."

"With guns, if necessary?"

"It won't be necessary."

"Possibly not to shoot anybody. The showin' mebbe'll turn the trick. Now, look here. My idea is that if a bunch of us fellows got together on the quiet some night an' seized a few elevators—Say, wouldn't it bring things to a head so quick we'd get action? The law's there, but these fellows are deliberately breakin' it an' we got to show 'em—"

"The action you'd get would be the wrong kind, Mac," protested W. R. Motherwell emphatically. "You'd land in jail!"

"Don't see it that way," persisted McNair. "Wouldn't give a continental if I did so long's it woke a few people up."

"I tell you you're on the wrong trail unless you want to get it where the chicken got the axe!"

"Doggone it, man! Ain't that where we're gettin' it *now*?"

"Whereas with the right kind of organization—"

"Don't believe it," grunted McNair, starting to climb back to his horse. "The time for any more o' these here granny tea-parties is past to my way o' thinkin' an' if we can't agree on it, we'd better shut up before we get mad." He vaulted easily into the saddle. "But I'll tell you one thing, W. R.—there's the sweetest little flare-up you ever saw on its way. I was talkin' the other day to Ed. Partridge, the Railton boys, Al. Quigley, Billy Bonner and some more—"

"And I'll bet they gave you a lot of sound advice, Mac!" laughed Motherwell confidently.

"That's alright," resented McNair, the tan of his cheek

deepening a trifle. "They're a pretty sore bunch an' a fellow from down Turtle Mountain way in Manitoba told me—"

"That the mud-turtle and the jack-rabbit finally agreed that slow and steady—"

"Bah! You're sure hopeless," grinned the owner of the Two-Bar, giving his horse the rein.

"Hope*ful*," corrected W. R. Motherwell with a laugh. "Tell Wilson, if you see him, that Peter Dayman and I are expecting him over next week, will you? And I say, Mac, don't kill too many before you get home!" he called in final jocularity.

The flying horseman waved his hat and his "S'long" came back faintly. The other watched till horse and rider lost themselves among the distant wheat stocks. The twinkle died out of his eyes as he watched.

So McNair was another of them, eh? After all, that was only to be expected of an old Indian fighter and cow-puncher like him. Poor Bob! He had his reputation to sustain among the newcomers—hard rider, hard fighter, hard drinker; to do it under the changed conditions naturally required some hard talking on occasion. While Mac had become civilized enough to keep one foot in a cowhide boot planted in the practical present, the other foot was still moccasined and loath to forget the days of war-paint and whiskey-traders, feathers and fears. Over the crudities and hardships, the dirt and poverty, the years between had hung a kindly curtain of glamor; so that McNair with his big soft kerchiefs, his ranger's hat, his cow-puncher's saddle and trappings and his "Two-Bar" brand was a figure to crane an Eastern neck.

Likeable enough chap—too much of a man to be treated as a

joke to his face, but by no means to be taken seriously—not on most occasions. In the present instance, with feeling running as high as it was in some quarters, that crazy idea of seizing a few elevators at the point of a gun—! What in heaven's name would they do with them after they got them? Nevertheless, McNair might find rattle-brained listeners enough to cause a heap of trouble. There were always a few fellows ready for excitement; they might go in for the fun of it, then before they knew it the thing would curdle over night like a pan of milk in a thunder-storm.

"He's just darn fool enough to try some funny work," muttered the anxious driver of the grain wagon. "Jailing him only makes a hero of him and that's the kind of thing the beggar glories in. The son-of-a-gun!"

One by one throughout the afternoon the miles crept tediously beneath the wagon. The sun which had steeped the stubble in gold all day had turned the sky and was poising for its nightly dip below the horizon by the time the long misty blue line of the Qu'Appelle hills began to creep from the prairie. When the lone traveller at last could count the deep shadowy coulees the sun had disappeared, but the riot of after-fires still burned brightly in the west. He had passed his own place hours before, but had stopped there only for a change of horses and a brief rest; a parcel and an important message which he wished to deliver in person at Fort Qu'Appelle without delay was extending his day's journey.

Six hundred feet below the level of the plain the grassy slopes of the Qu'Appelle Valley bowled to the blue lakes. Hugging the water's edge, the buildings of the romantic old fort scattered in the twilight. The winding trail stood out like a white thread that reached down the valley towards the Catholic Mission of Lebret.

Before heading into the steep descent the farmer from over Abernethy way slipped on his heavy cardigan jacket; for behind the rim of the hills the sunset fires were dying and already the coolness of the October night was making itself felt. At the mouth of a coulee he spoke to a solitary Indian, standing motionless before a camp fire. The appetizing odor of roasting wild fowl reminded him that he was more than ready for the "bite to eat" which he would enjoy with the good Father Hugonard at the Indian Mission—he of the dark, gentle eyes, the quick understanding, the quiet tones. There would be much to talk about.

So it proved. The hour was growing late when finally he bade good-bye to his pleasant host and resumed his journey in the starlight, refreshed and encouraged. For here in the seclusion of this peaceful valley, since the days of the great buffalo herds, Father Hugonard had ministered to the Indians, starved with them, worked patiently with them through many seasons of flowers and snows. Nevertheless, out of many discouragements and privations had this sterling man retained an abiding faith in the triumph of righteousness in all things.

In the quiet beauty of the wonderful October night was little place for the anxious thoughts of the day. Bitterness of spirit, the bickerings of men, commercial Oppression and injustice—these were things far removed from the planets of the Ages that sparkled like jewels in the vault of Night. A vagrant breeze whispered in the valley sedges to the placid lake. High in the air, invisible, migrating *wavies* winged into the south, the distant gabble of their passing falling weirdly earthward.

The trail began to ascend sharply. Off to the right the sky was growing rapidly lighter behind a distant hill and presently a lop of yellow moon crept slowly over the edge and rose into the air like a broken chalice, chasing the shadows to their retreats.

As he watched it the driver of the grain wagon recalled again the old Indian legend that haunted this valley and had given it its name—how, long ago, a young Indian chieftain was paddling his canoe through these waters on his way to win a bride when suddenly above "the night wind's melancholy song" he heard a voice calling him through the twilight. "Qu'appelle? Qu'appelle?" he answered in French. "Who calls?" But only his own voice came back in echoes while the gloom of night deepened and a wan moon rose silently behind the distant hill. Then when he reached the Indian encampment it was only to see the death fires lighted on the shore, to hear the wail of women and to learn that just before her lips had closed forever, his beloved had called for him— just at the moon-rise. Thus, ever since, the Indians claimed, strange spirit voices spoke through the lone valley at every rising of the moon.

Thrilled by the beauty of the valley scene, misty in the moonlight, the big farmer half unconsciously drew rein and listened. All he could hear at first was the impatient stamp of his horses' feet, the mouthing of the bits as the animals tossed their heads restlessly, the clink of the trace-chains; but presently he sensed a subdued undertone of night noises that wafted mysteriously over the silver water. It was nothing that could be recognized definitely; rather was it an impression of strangely merged minor sounds that grew upon him as imagination was given play under the influence of time and place. It was easy to supply interpretations of that faint medley, even while one knew that it was merely the murmur of night airs in the dry grasses, the whisper of the water-edges, the stirring of restless water-fowl in the dying reeds.

The man who had ridden all day with his thoughts began

unconsciously to apply other meanings to the sound, to people the night with dim faces and shapes that came trooping over the edge of the tablelands above—toil-bent figures of old pioneer farmers, care-worn faces of women and bright eager faces of little children who were holding out their hands trustfully to the future. There seemed to be a never-ending procession—faces that were apathetic from repeated disappointments, faces that scowled threateningly, brave faces tense with determination and sad faces on which was written the story of struggle hidden within many a lonely wind-buffeted shack on the great bosom of the prairie.

Was it, then, that all the years of toil and hardship were to come to naught for this great company of honest workers, these brave pioneer men and women of the soil? Was all their striving forward to find them merely marking time, shouldered into the backwater while the currents of organized commercialism swept away their opportunities? Were not these producers of the world's bread themselves to partake of the fruits of their labor?

Yes! Surely the answer was *Yes!* It was their Right. Wrong could not endure forever in the face of Right; else were the world a poor place, Life itself a failure, the mystic beauty of God's calm night a mockery.

The man from Abernethy roused himself. It would be nearly dawn before his team would reach their home stalls. He whistled to the horses and they plunged into the black shadows of the coulee up which the trail rose in steep ascent from the valley. When they emerged into the moonlight he drew rein for a moment.

Somewhere back in a forgotten arroyo a coyote yapped lonesomely. Around through the night were flung the distant glow-dots of the burning straw piles, and as he filled his

Hopkins Moorhouse

lungs with the fresh sweet air the hope of better days warmed the heart of the belated traveller. The Hand which set the orbits of the universe created the laws of Truth and Justice and these never could be gainsaid. Everything would come out aright if only men were steadfast in faith and duty.

He gave the horses their heads and they were off once more through the cool night upon the wheatland sea that was bounded only by far purple shadows.

[1] The provinces of Saskatchewan and Alberta, Western Canada, were not created until 1906. Prior to that the entire country west of the Province of Manitoba was known as the North-West Territories, of which the District of Assiniboia was a part, the part which subsequently formed the southern portion of the Province of Saskatchewan.

[2] Hon. W. R. Motherwell, Minister of Agriculture, Province of Saskatchewan.

CHAPTER II

A CALL TO ARMS

And my hand hath found as a nest the riches of the people: and as one gathereth eggs that are left, have I gathered all the earth.

—Isaiah 10:14.

For five thousand years Man has grown wheat for food. Archaeologists have found it buried with the mummies of Egypt; the pictured stones of the Pyramids record it. But it was the food of princes, not of peasants—of the aristocracy, not of the people; for no man could harvest enough of it with his sickle to create a supply which would place it within the reach of the poor. While century after century[1] has passed since wheat was first recognized as the premier nourishment for the human body, it is only of recent times that it has become the food of the nations.

The swift development of grain growing into the world's greatest industry goes back for a small beginning to 1831. It was in that year that a young American-born farm boy of Irish-Scotch extraction was jeered and laughed at as he attempted to cut wheat with the first crude reaper; but out of Cyrus Hall McCormick's invention soon grew the wonderful harvesting machinery which made possible the production of wheat for export. Close on heel the railways and water-carriers began competing for the transportation of the grain, the railways pushing eagerly in every direction where new wheat lands could be tapped. In 1856 wheat was leaving Chicago for Europe and four years later grain vessels from California were rounding Cape Horn. The nine years that followed saw the conquest of the vast prairies of the American West which were crossed by the hissing, iron monsters that stampeded the frightened bison, out-ran the wild horses and out-stayed the lurking Indian.

No sooner had the railways pushed back the frontier than wheat began to trickle steadily upon the market, to flow with increased volume, then to pour in by train-loads. Sacks were discarded for quicker shipment in bulk; barns and ware-houses filled and spilled till adequate storage facilities became the vital problem and, the need mothering invention, F. H. Peavey came forward with an idea—an endless chain of metal cups for elevating grain. From this the huge modern elevator evolved to take its place as the grain's own particular storehouse. With the establishment of exchanges for conducting international buying and selling the universa-lizing of wheat was complete.

These things had come to pass while that great region which is now Western Canada was still known as a Great Lone Land. Pioneer settlers, however, were beginning to venture westward to the newly organized Province of Manitoba and beyond. The nearest railroad was at St. Paul, Minnesota, from which point a "prairie schooner" trail led north for 450 miles to Winnipeg at the junction of the Red and Assiniboine rivers; the alternative to this overland tented-wagon route was a tedious trip by Red River steamer. It was not until 1878 that a railway was built north into Manitoba from St. Paul; but it was followed shortly after by the projection of the Canadian

Pacific Railway, which reached Vancouver in 1886.

Then began what has been called the greatest wheat-rush ever known. Land, land without end, to be had for the asking—rich land that would grow wheat, forty bushels to the acre, millions of acres of it! Fabulous tales, winging east and south, brought settlers pouring into the new country. They came to grow wheat and they grew it, the finest wheat in the world. They grew it in ever increasing volume.

Successful operation of new railroads—even ordinary railroads—is not all glistening varnish and bright new signal flags. The Canadian Pacific was no ordinary railway. It was a young giant, reaching for the western skyline with temerity, and it knew Trouble as it knew sun and wind and snow. The very grain which was its life-blood gorged the embryo system till it choked. The few elevators and other facilities provided could not begin to handle the crop, even of 1887, the heavy yield upsetting all calculations. The season for harvesting and marketing being necessarily short, the railroad became the focus of a sudden belch of wheat; it required to be rushed to the head of the lakes in a race with the advancing cold which threatened to congeal the harbor waters about the anxiously waiting grain boats before they could clear. With every wheel turning night and day no ordinary rolling stock could cope with the demands; for the grain was coming in over the trails to the shipping points faster than it could be hauled out and the railroad was in a fix for storage accommodation.

It was easy to see that such seasonal rushes would be a permanent condition in Western Canada, vital but unavoidable; so the Canadian Pacific Railway Company cast about for alleviations. They hit upon the plan of increasing storage facilities rapidly by announcing that the Company would make special concessions to anyone who would build elevators along the line with a capacity of not less than 26,000 bushels and equipped with cleaning machinery, steam or gasoline power—in short, "standard" elevators. The special inducement offered was nothing more nor less than an agreement that at points where such elevators were erected the railway company would not allow cars to be loaded with grain through flat warehouses, direct from farmers' vehicles or in any other way than through such elevators; the only "condition" was that the elevator owners would furnish storage and shipping facilities, of course, for those wishing to store or ship grain.

At once the noise of hammer and saw resounded along the right-of-way. Persons and corporations whose business it was to mill grain, to buy and export it, were quick to take advantage of the opportunity; for the protection offered by the railway meant that here was shipping control of the grain handed out on a silver platter, garnished with all the delectable prospects of satisfying the keenest money hunger.

On all sides protests arose from the few owners of ordinary warehouses who found their buildings useless, once the overtopping elevator went up alongside—from small buyers who found themselves being driven out of the market with the flat warehouses. But these voices were drowned in the swish of grain in the chutes and the staccato of the elevator engines—lost in the larger exigencies of the wheat. The railway company held to their promises and the tall grain boxes reared their castor tops against the sky in increasing clusters.

To operate a standard elevator at a country point with profit it was considered necessary in the early days to fill it three times in a season unless the owner proposed to deal in grain himself and make a buyer's profit in addition to handling grain for others. The cost of building and operating the class of elevator demanded by the railway company was partly responsible for this. Before long the number of elevators in Manitoba and the North-West Territories increased till it was impossible for all of them to obtain the three fillings per season even had their owners been inclined to perform merely a handling service.

But those who had taken up the railway's offer with such avidity and had invested large sums of shareholders' capital in building the elevator accommodation were mostly shrewd grain dealers whose primary object was to buy and sell. These interested corporations were not constructing elevators in order to admire their silhouettes against the beautiful prairie sunsets! In every corner of the earth the Dollar Almighty, or its equivalent, was being stalked by all sorts and conditions of men, some of whom chased it noisily and openly while others hunted with their boots in one hand. Properly enough, the grain men were out for all that their investment could earn and for all the wheat which they could buy at one price and sell at another. That was their business, just as it was the business of the railway company to transport the grain at a freight rate which would net a profit, just as it was the farmer's business—

But to the farmer it seemed that he had no business! He merely grew the grain. Apparently a farmer was a pair of pants, a shirt and a slouch hat that sat on a wagon-load of wheat, drove it up the incline into the elevator and rattled away again for another load! To farm was an occupation easily parsed—subjunctive mood, past tense, passive voice! The farmer was third person, singular! He came and went in single file like an Indian or a Chinaman—John Doe, Yon Yonson and Johann X (his mark)—every kind of Johnny on no spot but his own! As soon as his grain was dumped each of him went back to the land among the dumb animals where the pomp and vanity of this wicked world would not interfere with preparations for next year's crop!

Wheat was bought upon the grading system—so much per bushel for this grade, so much for that, according to the fluctuations of supply and demand upon the world's markets. But the average farmer at that time knew little or nothing about what went on in the great exchanges of the cities; there was no means of learning the intricacies of the grain business and many farmers even did not know what a grain exchange was. All such a man knew was that his wheat was graded and he received a certain price for it.

The railway company's refusal to furnish cars for loading direct from the farmer's wagon compelled the shipper to sell to the elevator operator for whatever price he could get, accepting whatever weights the operator allowed and whatever "dockage" he chose to decree. The latter represented that portion of the farmer's delivery which was supposed to come through the cleaning sieves as waste material such as dirt, weed seeds, broken wheat kernels, etc. To determine the percentage of dockage in any given load of wheat the ordinary human being would require to weigh and clean a pound of it at least; but so expert were many of the elevator operators of those days that they had no trouble at all in arriving at the dockage by a single glance. Nor were they disconcerted by the fact that the country was new and grain frequently came from the thresher in a remarkably clean condition.

With everything thus fallow for seeds of discord the Big Trouble was not long in making itself manifest. All over the country the Bumping of the Bumpkins apparently became the favorite pastime of elevator men. Certain persons with most of their calluses on the inside cracked the whip and the three-ring circus began. Excessive dockage, short weights, depressed prices! The farmers grew more and more bitter as time passed. To begin with, they resented being compelled by the railway to deal with the elevators; it was a violation of that liberty which they had a right to enjoy as British citizens. The grain was theirs to sell where they liked, and when on top of the refusal to let them do it came this bleeding of their crops, their indignation was fanned to white heat.

It was useless for the farmers to build elevators of their own; for these had to conform to the requirements of the railway and, as already stated, it was impossible to run them profitably without making a buyer's profit in addition to the commission for handling and storage. The farmers were not buyers but sellers of grain and with very few exceptions, where conditions were specially favorable, the farmers' elevators that were attempted were soon in difficulties.

Leading farmers began to write strong letters to the newspapers and it was not long before the agitation became so widespread that it reached the floor of Parliament. Mr. James M. Douglas, member for East Assiniboia, during two successive sessions introduced Bills to regulate the shipping and transportation of grain in Manitoba and the North-West Territories and these were discussed in the House of Commons. A Special Committee of the House was appointed finally to investigate the merits of the case and as considerable difference of opinion was expressed as to the actual facts, the appointment of a Royal Commission to make a full and impartial investigation of the whole subject in the public interest was recommended.

This Royal Commission accordingly was appointed on October 7th, 1899, and consisted of three Manitoba farmers—W. F. Sirett, of Glendale; William Lothian, of Pipestone, and Charles C. Castle, of Foxton—with His Honor E. J. Senkler, of St. Catharines, Ontario, as Chairman; Charles N. Bell, of

Winnipeg, acted as Secretary. Owing to the illness and death of Judge Senkler, Albert Elswood Richards (afterwards the late Hon. Mr. Justice Richards, of Winnipeg), succeeded as Chairman in February, 1900.

Sittings were held at many places throughout Manitoba and the North-West Territories and much evidence was taken as to the grievances complained of, these being mainly: (1) That vendors of grain were being subjected to unfair and excessive dockage at the time of sale; (2) That doubt existed as to the fairness of the weights allowed or used by owners of elevators; (3) That the owners of elevators enjoyed a monopoly in the purchase of grain by refusing to permit the erection of flat warehouses where standard elevators were situated and were thus able to keep prices of grain below true value to their own benefit and the disadvantage of the public generally as well as others who were specially interested in the grain trade.

Meanwhile the railway companies had hastened to announce that they would furnish cars to farmers who wished to ship direct and do their own loading. This concession, made in 1898-9, resulted in somewhat better prices and better treatment from the elevator operators. But farmers who lived more than four or five miles from the shipping points could not draw in their grain fast enough to load a car within the time allowed by the railway; so that the situation, so far as these farmers were concerned, remained practically unchanged.

In March, 1900, the Royal Commission made a complete report. They had done their work thoroughly. They found that so long as any farmer was hampered in shipping to terminal markets himself he would be more or less at the mercy of elevator operators and that the only proper relief from the possibility of undue dockage and price depression was to be found in the utmost freedom of shipping and selling. To this end they considered that the railroads should be compelled by law to furnish farmers with cars for shipping their own grain and that flat warehouses should be allowed so that the farmer could have a bin in which to accumulate a carload of grain, if he so wished. This, the commissioners thought, should be the farmer's legal right rather than his privilege. Loading platforms for the free use of shippers were also recommended.

It was the further opinion of the Commission that the law should compel elevator and warehouse owners to guarantee the grades and weights of a farmer's grain and to do this the adoption of a uniform grain ticket system was suggested. At the same time, the commissioners pointed out, these guarantees might lead to such careful grading and docking by the elevator operator as might appear to the farmer to be undergrading or overdocking; so that the farmer's right to load direct on cars was a necessary supplementary protection.

The annual shortage of cars during the rush season following harvest was found to be a direct cause of depression in prices. When cars were not available for immediate shipments the grain soon piled up on the elevator companies who were thereby forced to miss the cheaper transportation by boat from the head of the lakes or assume the risk of carrying over the grain until the following spring; in buying, therefore, they naturally allowed a wide margin to cover all possible contingencies. Increase of transportation facilities during October and November accordingly was imperative.

With no rules to regulate the grain trade except those laid down by the railways and the elevator owners, the need was great for definite legislation similar to that which obtained in the State of Minnesota and, as a result of the Royal

Commission's recommendations, the Manitoba Grain Act was placed upon the statutes and became operative in 1900. To supervise the carrying out of the law in connection with the grain trade a Warehouse Commissioner was appointed, Mr. C. C. Castle who acted on the Royal Commission being selected for this responsible office.

A sigh of relief went up from many intelligent farmers who had begun to worry over the conditions developing; for they looked upon the Manitoba Grain Act as a sort of Magna Charta. With the grain trade under official control and supervision along the lines laid down by the Royal Commission, they felt that everything would be alright now. It was like calling in a policeman to investigate suspicious noises in the house; like welcoming the doctor's arrival upon an occasion of sudden and severe illness. Unfortunately, the patient's alarming symptoms sometimes continue; sometimes the thief makes a clean get-away; King John had no sooner left Runnymede than he proceeded to ignore the Great Charter and plan new and heavier scutages upon the people!

Up till now the elevator owners had been operating with nothing more definite than a fellowship of interests to hold them together; but upon appearance of the Grain Act they proceeded to organize the North West Elevator Association, afterwards called the North West Grain Dealers' Association. By agreeing on the prices which they would pay for wheat out in the country and by pooling receipts the members of such an organization, the farmers suspected, would be in a position to strangle competition in buying.

The new Act was aiming point blank at these very things by affording the farmer an opportunity of loading his grain direct into cars through flat warehouses, if he chose, and shipping where he liked. But because many farmers did not know with just what the new weapon was loaded or how to pull the trigger, the railways and elevators merely stepped up and smilingly brushed the whole thing aside as something which were better hanging on a high peg out of harm's way.

The crop of 1900 being comparatively light, the ignoring of the car-distribution clauses of the Act did not obtrude as brazenly as it did the year following. But when grain began to pour in to the shipping points in 1901 and the farmers found the railway unheeding their requests for cars their disgust and disappointment were as complete as their anger was swift. It was the rankling disappointment of men whose rights have been officially decreed only to be unofficially annulled; it was the hot anger of a slap in the face—the anger that makes men fight with every ounce of their strength.

The quick welling of it planted anxiety in the minds of such level-headed farmers as W. R. Motherwell and Peter Dayman, of Abernethy; Williams, of Balcarres; Snow, of Wolseley; Sibbold and Millar, of Indian Head. While the two latter were riding into town with wheat one day John Sibbold suggested to John Millar that, as secretary of the local Agricultural Society, it might be a good thing if he called a meeting to talk things over. It was the high state of feeling manifested at this meeting which furnished W. R. Motherwell with food for thought on the lonely Qu'Appelle trail. And it was the idea that it might be advisable to hold similar mass meetings throughout the country that brought Peter Dayman driving over to the Motherwell place, not long after, to discuss it.

These two men had been friends and neighbors since 1883. Each of them felt that the time had come for definite action of some kind and they spent the greater part of the day in talking over the situation in search of the most practical plan of campaign. There was little use in the farmers attempting to organize in defence of their own interests unless the effort were absolutely united and along broader lines than those of any previous farmers' organization. Politics, they both agreed, would have to be kept out of the movement at all costs or it would land on the rocks of defeat in the same way that the Farmers' Union and Patrons of Industry had been wrecked.

It was in the middle eighties when the West was settled but sparsely that the farmers had attempted to improve their lot by the formation of "Farmers' Unions." The movement had had a brief and not very brilliant career and as the offspring of this attempt at organization some progressives with headquarters at Brandon, Manitoba, had tried to enter the grain trade as an open company. When one of the chief officers of this concern defected in an attempt to get rich the failure dragged down the earnest promoters to deep financial losses.

Again in the early nineties the farmers had rebelled at their pioneer hardships by organizing the "Patrons of Industry," a movement which had gained strength and for a while looked healthy. It had got strong enough to elect friends to the Legislature and was sowing good seed when again temptation appeared, centred in the lure of commercial success and politics. Some of the chief officers began to misuse the organization for selfish ends and away went the whole thing.

There was no use in repeating these defeats. Couldn't some way be devised of sidestepping such pitfalls? The great weakness of the farmers was their individual independence; if they could be taught to stand together for their common interests there was hope that something might be accomplished.

The sitting-room clock ticked away the hours unheeded as

these two far-sighted and conscientious farmers lost themselves in earnest discussion. The lamps were lighted, but still they planned.

Finally W. R. Motherwell reached across the table for a pad of note-paper and drafted the call to arms—a letter which summoned the men of Wolseley, Sintaluta and Indian Head, of Qu'Appelle, Wideawake and other places to gather for *action*. There and then copies were written out for every leading farmer within reach, and in order that no political significance might be attached to the call, both men signed the letters.

When Peter Dayman drove away from the Motherwell place that night perhaps he scarcely realized that he carried in his pocket the fate of the farmers of Western Canada. Neither he, W. R. Motherwell, nor any other man could have foretold the bitter struggles which those letters were destined to unleash—the stirring events that were impending.

[1] Wheat was first grown in Canada in 1606 at Port Royal (now Annapolis) in Nova Scotia, where Champlain and Pourtincourt built a fort and established a small colony. A plot of ground was made ready and wheat planted. "It grew under the snow," said Pourtincourt, "and in the following midsummer it was harvested."

CHAPTER III

THE FIRST SHOT IS FIRED

Let us have faith that Right makes Might, and in that faith let us dare to do our duty as we understand it.

—Abraham Lincoln.

The eighteenth of December, 1901, was a memorable day in the little prairie town of Indian Head. Strangers from East and West had begun to arrive the night before and early in the day the accommodations were taxed to the limit while the livery stables were overflowing with the teams of farmers from every direction. All forenoon the trails were dotted with incoming sleighs and the groups which began to congregate on Main Street grew rapidly in size and number. The shop-keepers had stayed up half the night to put the final touches to their holiday decorations and make their final preparations for the promised rush of Christmas buying.

Many prominent men would grace the town with their presence before nightfall. The Premier of the North-West Territories, Hon. F. W. G. Haultain, would be on hand, as well as Hon. G. H. V. Bulyea and Senator William D. Perley; coming to meet them here would be Premier R. P. Roblin and other gentlemen of Manitoba. Certain boundary matters, involving the addition of a part of Assiniboia to the Province of Manitoba, were to be discussed at a public meeting in the Town Hall at night.

Messrs. Motherwell and Dayman had chosen their date well, many farmers having planned already to be at Indian Head on the 18th. The grain growers' meeting was announced for the afternoon and so keen was the interest that when order was called the chairman faced between sixty and seventy-five farmers, as well as a number of public men, instead of the dozen-or-so whom W. R. Motherwell had ventured to expect.

Although it was December out of doors, the temperature of that meeting was about one hundred in the shade! As the discussion expanded feeling ran high. Farmer after farmer got to his feet and told the facts as he knew them, his own personal experiences and those of his neighbors. There was no denying the evidence that it was full time the farmers bestirred themselves.

W. R. Motherwell and Peter Dayman spoke earnestly in favor of immediate organization along strong, sane lines. The farmer was always referred to as the most independent man on earth, and so he was; but it was individual independence only. He had come lumbering into the country behind his own oxen with his family and all his worldly goods in his own wagon; had built a roof over their heads with his own hands. Alone on the prairie, he had sweated and wrestled with the problem of getting enough to eat. One of the very first things the pioneer learned was to stand on his own two feet—to do things by himself. His isolation, the obstacles he had overcome by his own planning, the hardships he had endured and survived—these were the excuses for his assertiveness, his individualism, his hostility to the restrictions of organization. He was a horse for work; but it was an effort for him to do team work because he was not used to it.

This was the big barrier which would have to be surmounted in the beginning if battle were to be waged successfully against present oppressive conditions. The right kind of organization was the key that would unlock a happier future. The farmer was as much a producer as any manufacturer who made finished articles out of raw material; but his was the only business in which full energies were expended upon production of goods to sell while the marketing end was left for the "other fellow" to organize. That was why he was obliged to do as he was told, take what was given him or haul his wheat home and eat it himself.

Like all such meetings, it was not without its few pails of cold water. These were emptied by some who hinted dark things about "political reasons," and it was easy to make the trite statement that history repeats itself and to predict that the formation of such a farmers' association as was proposed would be riding only for the same fall which had overtaken former attempts. The enthusiasm refused to be dampened and it broke out in unmistakable accents when without waste of words Angus McKay nominated W. R. Motherwell as provisional President of the "Territorial Grain Growers' Association." John Millar as provisional Secretary and a board of directors[1] were quickly chosen.

When it was all over and Senator William D. Perley rose slowly to his feet, it was to deliver a parting message of confidence that the farmers were taking the right step in the right manner. There were few men who could be listened to with greater respect than the elderly Senator and as the silence of his audience deepened it was almost as if the white-haired gentleman's dignified words were prophetic. He had been familiar with a somewhat similar movement in New Brunswick, he said, and back there by the Atlantic this movement was still very much alive and doing good work. Long after those who were present at this meeting had passed away, it was his prediction that this newborn organization of prairie farmers would be living still, still expanding and still performing a useful service to the farmers generally.

The meeting adjourned with the general feeling that at last matters were advancing beyond mere talk. The sixth of January was set as the date for a second meeting to draft a constitution and prepare a definite plan of campaign. Emphasis was laid upon the importance of a good attendance; but when the date arrived the leaders of the new movement were disappointed to find that, including themselves, there were just eleven farmers present. While this did not look very promising, they proceeded with their plans and it is a tribute to the careful thought expended at that time that the constitution then framed has stood the test of many years, even much of the exact phraseology remaining to-day. The idea of having local associations scattered throughout the country, each with its own officers, governed by a central organization with its special officers, was adopted from the first.

Among those present was C. W. Peterson, Deputy Commissioner of Agriculture for the North-West Territories. He freely offered his services in the capacity of secretary; but the offer was turned down so flat and so quickly that it was breath-taking. The incident reflected very vividly the jealousy with which the farmers were guarding the new movement rather than any depreciation of the Deputy Commissioner's ability; every man of them was on the alert to deflect the thinnest political wedge, imagined or otherwise, that might come along. They would trust nobody with an official connection and the appointment of John Millar, who was one of themselves, was confirmed without loss of time. There was no salary attached to any office, of course; nobody thought of salaries. The farmers who knew the feel of spare cash in those days were seventh sons of seventh sons.

Winter and all as it was, the leaders of the young organization did not let the snow pack under their feet. No sooner were the preliminaries over than they set about preparing for the first convention of the Association by hitching up and travelling the country, organizing local associations. W. R. Motherwell, John Millar and Matt. Snow, of Wolseley, tucked the robes around them and jingled away in different directions. Wherever they went they were listened to eagerly and the resulting action was instantaneous. The movement took hold of the farmers like wildfire; so that by February thirty-eight local grain growers' associations had been formed, each sending enthusiastic delegates to the first Annual Convention, which was held at Indian Head in February, 1902.

All that summer, pacing the rapidly growing wheat, the Territorial Grain Growers' Association spread and took root till by harvest time it was standing everywhere in the field, a thrifty and full-headed champion of farmers' rights, lacking only the ripening of experience. There had been as yet no particular opportunity to demonstrate its usefulness in dollars and cents; but with the approach of the fall and market season the whole organization grew tense with expectancy. There seemed little reason to believe that the railway people would do other than attempt to continue their old methods of distributing cars where and when they chose and to disregard, as before, those provisions of the Grain Act which aimed to protect the farmer in getting his fair share of cars in which to load direct.

Thus it soon turned out. The officers of the Association at

once warned the Canadian Pacific Railway Company that if they persisted in such practice the farmers would be compelled to take legal action against them. It looked so much like the attack of a toddling child against a man full grown that the big fellow laughed good-naturedly. Who, pray, were the "Territorial Grain Growers' Association"?

"We represent the farmers of Western Canada," retorted the unabashed officers of the little organization "and we want what the law allows us as our right. What's more, we propose to get it!"

That was about the message which W. R. Motherwell and Peter Dayman went down to Winnipeg to deliver in person to the Canadian Pacific Railway Company. The official whom they interviewed manipulated the necessary levers to start the matter on its way through the "proper channels" towards that "serious consideration" into which all good politicians and corporation officials take everything that comes unexpectedly before them. W. R. Motherwell could not wait for the unfolding of this hardy perennial and left Peter Dayman at Winnipeg to follow up developments.

When the latter got back home he brought with him a bagful of promises. The practical improvement in the situation which was to support these promises, however, evidently got wrapped up in somebody else's order and delivered to another address. As soon as the Association were satisfied that relief was not to be forthcoming they promptly filled out a standard form of information and complaint and notified the railway that they were going to take legal action at Sintaluta against the Company's station agent; if no results were forthcoming there, they assured the Company, they would take action against every railway agent in the Territories who was guilty of distributing cars contrary to the provisions of the Grain Act. The complaint went before Mr. C. C. Castle, the official

Warehouse Commissioner; the information was laid before Magistrate H. O. Partridge at Sintaluta.

All over the country the newspapers began to devote valuable space to the impending trial. It was talked about in bar-rooms and barber-shops. Some anti-railroaders declared at once that the farmers hadn't a minute's chance to win against the C. P. R. The news percolated eastward, its significance getting lighter till it became merely: "a bunch of fool hayseeds out West in some kind of trouble with the C. P. R.—cows run over, or something." At Ottawa, however, were those who saw handwriting on the wall and they awaited the outcome with considerable interest. Several public men, especially from Regina, made ready to be in actual attendance at the preliminary trial.

The farmers were out in force, for they realized the importance of this test case. It was not the agent at Sintaluta they were fighting, but the railway itself; it was not this specific instance of unjust car distribution that would be settled, but all other like infringements along the line. The very efficacy of the Grain Act itself was challenged.

Two hours before the Magistrate's Court sat to consider the case, J. A. M. Aikins (now Sir James Aikins, Lieutenant-Governor of Manitoba), who was there as the legal representative of the C. P. R., tapped the President of the farmers' Association on the elbow.

"Let's make a real case of it while we're at it," he smiled, and proceeded to suggest that instead of laying information against the railway company on two charges, the Association should charge them also with violating some five or six other sections of the Act. "Then we'll have a decision on them, too, you see. For the purpose of this case the Company will plead guilty to the offences. What do you say?"

"Don't you do it, W. R.! Not on your life, Mister!"

The farmers within earshot crowded about the two. They suspected trickery in such a last-minute suggestion; either the railway people were very sure they had the case in their pocket or they were up to some smooth dodge, you bet!

President Motherwell shook his head dubiously.

"How can we change the information on such short notice?" he objected. "It would mean risking an adjournment of the court."

"That's what they're after! Stick to him, Motherwell!"

But it did seem very advisable to have the meaning of those other doubtful sections of the Act cleared up, and as C. P. R. counsel went more fully into the matter the desirability of it for both sides became even more apparent.

"Tell you what we'll do, Mr. Aikins," said W. R. Motherwell, finally turning to him after consulting the others, "if you'll give your pledged word before this assembled crowd of farmers that you won't take any technical advantage of the change you've suggested us making in the information—by raising objections when court opens, I mean—why, we'll make the change."

"Certainly," agreed Mr. Aikins without hesitation, and in solemn silence he and the President of the Association shook hands.

This alteration in the information made the issue even more far-reaching and it was a tense moment for the farmers who packed the little court room when the Magistrate opened proceedings and on behalf of the Warehouse Commissioner,

Mr. T. Q. Mathers (now Chief Justice Mathers, of Winnipeg), rose to his feet for argument. After the evidence was complete and the Magistrate at last handed down his decision—fifty dollars fine and costs, to be paid by the defendant—the victorious grain growers were jubilant and especially were the officers of the young Association proud of the outcome.

The case was carried to the Supreme Court by the Railway Company, which made every effort to have the decision of the lower court reversed. When the appeal case came to trial, much to the disgust and chagrin of the railway authorities and the corresponding elation of the farmers, the Magistrate's decision was sustained. At once the newspapers all over the country were full of it. Oracles of bar-room and barber-shop nodded their heads wisely; hadn't they said that even the C. P. R. couldn't win against organized farmers, backed up by the law of the land? Away East the news was magnified till it became: "The farmers out West have licked the C. P. R. in court and are threatening to tear up the tracks!" At Ottawa Members of Parliament dug into Hansard to see if they had said anything when the Manitoba Grain Act was passed.

Empty cars began to roll into Western sidings and they were not all spotted to suit the elevators but were for farmers who had signified a desire to load direct. It was unnecessary to carry out the threat of proceeding against every delinquent railway agent in the Territories; for the delinquencies were no longer deliberate. The book in which by turn the orders for cars were listed began to be a more honest record of precedence in distribution, as all good car-order books should be.

For the railway authorities were men of wide experience and ability, who knew when they were defeated and how to accept such defeat gracefully. It meant merely that the time had come to recognize the fact that there was a man inside the soil-grimed shirt. The farmer had won his spurs. While the railway people did not like the action of the Association in hauling them into court, in all fairness they were ready to admit that they had received full warning before such drastic action was taken.

If the railway officials began to regard the farmer in a new light, the latter on his part began to appreciate somewhat more fully the task which faced these energetic men in successfully handling the giant organization for which they assumed responsibility. After the tilt, therefore, instead of the leaders of the grain growers and the railway looking at each other with less friendly eyes, their relations became more kindly as each began to entertain for the other a greater respect.

Best of all, applications were beginning to pour in upon the Secretary of the Territorial Grain Growers' Association— applications from farmers everywhere for admission to the organization. Skeptics who had been holding out now enrolled with their local association and, as fast as they could be handled, new locals were being formed.

And at this very time, over in the hotel at Sintaluta, a grain grower of great ability and discernment was warning an interested group of farmers against the dangers of over-confidence.

"At present we are but pygmies attacking giants," declared E. A. Partridge. "Giants may compete with giants, pygmies with pygmies, but pygmies with giants, never. We are not denizens of a hamlet but citizens of a world and we are facing the interlocking financial, commercial and industrial interests of a thousand million people. If we are to create a fighting force by co-operation of the workers to meet the giants created by the commercial co-operation of the owners, we have scarcely started. If we seek permanent improvement in our financial position and thereby an increase of comfort, opportunity and sense of security in our lives and the lives of our families, the fight will be long and hard.

"And we are going to need every man we can muster."

[1] See Appendix—Par. 1.

CHAPTER IV

"THAT MAN PARTRIDGE!"

Any man can work when every stroke of his hand brings down the fruit rattling from the tree to the ground; but to labor in season and out of season, under every discouragement, by the power of faith . . . that requires a heroism which is transcendent. And no man, I think, ever puts the plow into the furrow and does not look back, and sows good seed therein, that a harvest does not follow.

—Henry Ward Beecher.

It was a handy place to live, that little tar-paper shanty around which the prairie wind whooed and whiffed with such disdain. So small was it that it was possible to wash oneself, dress oneself and get breakfast without getting out of bed. On the wall was a shelf which did duty as a table. There were also a little box stove and some odds and ends. When the roof leaked, which was every time it rained, it was necessary to put pans on the bed to catch the drip.

But it was better than the tent in which E. A. Partridge and his brother slept through their first star-strewn winter nights on the open prairie—more pretentious than the tent and assuredly not so cold. The two boys were proud of it, even though they were fresh from civilization—from Simcoe County, Ontario, where holly-hocks topped the fences of old-fashioned flower gardens in summer and the houses had shingles on top to keep out the weather, and where there were no coyotes to howl lonesomely at night, where—Well, never mind. Those houses belonged to other people; the shanty was theirs. All around stretched acres and acres of snow; but there was land under that snow—rich, new land— and that was theirs, too, by right of homesteading.

It was about Christmas time in 1883 when E. A. Partridge was twenty-one. The place was near Sintaluta, District of Assiniboia, North-West Territories, and homesteading there in the days before the Rebellion was no feather bed for those who tackled it. A piece of actual money was a thing to take out and look at every little while, to show to one's friends and talk about.

Season after season the half starved agricultural pathfinders lost their hard-earned crops by drouth and what was not burned out by the sun was eaten by ubiquitous gophers. The drouth was due, no doubt, to the frequent prairie fires which swept the country; these found birth in the camp-fire coals left by ignorant or careless settlers on their way in. Under the rays of the summer sun the blackened ground became so hot that from it ascended a column of scorching air which interfered with the condensation of vapor preceding the falling of rain. Clouds would bank up above the prairie horizon, eagerly watched by anxious homesteaders; but over the burned area the clouds seemed to thin out without a drop falling upon the parching crops.

Forty-three acres, sown to wheat, was the first crop which the Partridge brothers put in. The total yield was seven bushels, obtained from around the edges of a slough!

One by one discouraged settlers gathered together their few belongings and sought fresh trails. Lone men trudged by, pack on back, silent and grim. Swearing at his horses, wheels squealing for axle-grease, tin pans rattling and flashing in the hot morning sun, a settler with a family stopped one day to ask questions of the two young men. He was on his way—somewhere—no place in particular.

"I tell ye, boys, this country ain't no place fer a white man," he volunteered. "When y'ain't freezin' ye're burnin' up, an' that's what happens in hell!" He spat a stream of tobacco juice over the wagon wheel and clawed his beard, his brown face twisted quizzically. "God A'mighty ain't nowheres near here! He didn't come this fur West—stopped down to Rat Portage![1] Well, anyways, good luck to ye both; but ef ye don't git it, young fellers, don't ye go blamin' me, by Jupiter!" He cracked his whip. "Come up out o' that, ye God-forsaken old skates!" And, mud-caked wheels screeching, tin pans banging and glaring, he jolted back to the trail that led away in distance to No Place In Particular.

But along with some others who confessed to being poor walkers, the Partridge boys stuck right where they were. They set about the building of a more permanent and comfortable shack—a sod house this time. It took more than seven thousand sods, one foot by three, three inches thick; but when it was finished it was a precocious raindrop or a mendacious wind that could find its way in.

About thirteen miles distant was a little mud schoolhouse, and one day E. A. Partridge was asked to go over and teach in it. It was known that back East, besides working on his father's farm, he had taught school for awhile. Learning was a truant for the younger generation on the prairies at that time, there being only a few private schools scattered here and there. Though it was not much of an opportunity for anything but something to do, the offer was accepted, and every morning, after sucking a couple of eggs for a breakfast, E. A. Partridge took to loping across the prairie on a "Shag" pony.

But the little school put an idea into his head. He wondered if it might be worth while starting a private school of his own, and in 1885 he thought the Broadview locality offered profitable prospects. He decided to go down there and look over the situation.

By this time the occupants of the sod house numbered four—three Partridge brothers and a friend. The problem of fitting out the school-teacher for his Broadview trip so that he would create the necessary impression among strangers was one which called for corrugated brows. The solution of it was not to be found in any of the teacher's few text-books; it quite upset Euclid's idea that things which were equal to the same thing were equal to one another—when it came to finding enough parts to make a respectable whole! For among the four bachelors was not one whole suit of clothes sufficiently presentable for social events. Everything was rough and ready in those days and in spite of the hardships the friendly pioneer settlers had some good times together; but the sod house quartette had never been seen at any of these gatherings—not all four at one time! Three of them were always so busy with this or that work that they had to stay home, you know; it would have been embarrassing to admit that it was only by pooling their clothes they could take turns in exhibiting a neighborly spirit. As it was, there was often a secret fear of exhibiting even more—an anxiety which led the visitor to keep the wall at his back like a man expecting general excitement to break loose at any moment!

On reaching Broadview the prospects for the new school looked bright, so the hopeful pedagogue sent back word to the sod house to this effect.

"And don't you fellows forget to send my linen," he wrote jokingly. "Make the trunk heavy, too. I don't know how long it will have to represent my credit!"

When the trunk arrived it was so heavy that it took two men to carry it into the hotel. When in the secrecy of his own room E. A. Partridge ventured to look inside he found his few books, a pair of "jumper" socks—and a lot of stones! Also there was an old duster with a piece of paper pinned to it, advising: "Here's your linen!"

The Broadview school did not last long for the reason that the second North-West Rebellion broke out that year and the teacher joined the Yorkton Rangers. Fifty cents a day and grub was an alluring prospect; many a poor homesteader would have joined the ranks on active service for the grub alone, especially when the time of his absence was being allowed by the Government to apply on the term set for homestead duties before he could come into full possession of his land. Many farmers earned money, also, teaming supplies from the railway north to Battleford and Prince Albert.

In common with his fellow grain growers, the five years that followed were years of continuous struggle for E. A. Partridge. The railway came and the country commenced to settle quickly. The days of prairie fires that ran amuck gave way to thriving crops; but at thirty and forty cents per bushel the thriving of those who sowed them was another matter.

This man with the snappy blue eyes and caustic tongue was among the first to foresee "the rising colossus," the shadow of which was creeping slowly across the farmer's path, and he watched the "brewing menace" with growing concern.

With every ounce of his tremendous energy he resented the encroachment of Capital upon the liberties of Labor. Being of the people and temperamentally a democrat, he had a great yearning for the reorganization of society in the general interest. His championship in this direction earned him the reputation in some quarters of being full of "fads," a visionary. But his neighbors, who had toiled and suffered beside him through the years, knew "Ed." Partridge, man to man, and held him in high regard; they admired him for his human qualities, respected him for his abilities, and wondered at his theories. On occasion they, too, shook their heads doubtfully. They could not know the big part in their emancipation which this friend and neighbor of theirs was destined to play through many days of crisis. Not yet had the talley begun.

But events even now slowly were shaping. With the winning of their first clash the farmers' movement was achieving momentum. In the latter part of December, 1902, down in the town of Virden, Manitoba, a committee was appointed at a meeting of the Virden Agricultural Society, to arrange a district meeting for the purpose of organizing the first Grain Growers' Association in Manitoba. As soon as the date was set J. W. Scallion wrote to W. R. Motherwell, urgently asking him to assist in the organization. Although roads and weather were rough, the President of the Territorial Grain Growers' Association at considerable inconvenience went down to Virden, taking with him Matt. Snow and copies of the constitution and by-laws upon which the Territorial Association was founded, With this assistance a strong local association was formed at Virden on January 9th, 1903, with capable officers[2] and a first-year membership of one hundred and twenty-five.

The same difficulties that faced the farmers farther West were being experienced in Manitoba and the newspapers were full of protesting letters from country points. As President of the Virden Grain Growers' Association, J. W. Scallion wrote letters to every place where complaints were being voiced and urged organization. At every opportunity it was advocated through the press that from the eastern boundary of Manitoba to the Rocky Mountains the farmers should organize themselves for self-defence against oppression, present or possible, by "the interests." In about six weeks over fifteen local associations had been formed in Manitoba and Virden began calling for a Provincial association. Accordingly, on March 3rd and 4th, 1903, the Manitoba grain growers held their first convention at Brandon with one hundred delegates present, representing twenty-six local associations. Great enthusiasm marked the event and the officers[3] chosen were all men of initiative.

The members of the parent organization watched the rapid expansion on all sides with sparkling eyes. Their own second annual convention at Indian Head revealed considerable progress and the promise of greater things to come. On the invitation of the delegates from the Regina district it was decided to hold the third annual convention at the capital and the rousing gathering which met there in due course was productive of such stimulus and publicity that its effect was felt long afterward.

At every convention the farmers found some additional weak spot in the Grain Act and suggested remedial legislation. Records are lacking to show in what order the various changes came; but step by step the farmers were gaining their rights. It all seemed so wonderful—to get together thus and frame requests of the Government at Ottawa, to find their very wording incorporated in the Act. The farmers scarcely had dared to think of such a thing before. To them the ear of a government was a delicate organism beyond reach, attuned to the acoustics of High Places only; that it was an ear to hear, an ear to the ground to catch the voice of the people was a discovery. At any rate when W. R. Motherwell and J. B. Gillespie, of the Territories, D. W. McCuaig and R. C. Henders, of Manitoba, went to Ottawa for the first time they were received with every consideration and many of their requests on behalf of the farmers granted.

With such recognition and the recurring evidence of advantageous results the jeering grins of a certain section of the onlooking public began to sober down to a less disrespectful mien. Those who talked glibly at first of the other farmers' organizations which they had seen go to pieces became less free with their forebodings.

In 1904 the farmers began to press for something more than the proper distribution of cars and the freedom of shipment. They were dissatisfied with the grading system and the re-inspection machinery. Some of them claimed that the grading system did not classify wheat according to its milling value. Some wanted a change in the Government's staff at the office of the Chief Grain Inspector where the official grading was done. Some wanted a sample market; some didn't. The farmers were about evenly divided.

The Department of Agriculture for the Territories commi-ssioned Professor Robert Harcourt, Chemist of the Ontario Agricultural College, to conduct tests as to the comparative values of the different grades of wheat. E. A. Partridge, of Sintaluta, and A. A. Perley, of Wolseley, undertook to secure eight-bushel samples of the various grades from their districts. These were carefully sacked and shipped to the Chief Grain Inspector at Winnipeg, where he graded them and forwarded them to Professor Harcourt, sealed in such a way that any tampering with the shipment would be detected readily.

These samples were all of 1903 crop. There had been a bad

snowstorm in September of that year and much wheat had been standing in stook. The farmers believed that the grain was not frozen or injured in any way and that they were defrauded to some extent in the grading of their wheat. The samples represented all grades from "No. 1 Hard" to "Feed." They were milled with exceptional care to prevent mixing of the various lots and the flours obtained were put through three different baking tests.

The conclusion reached was that there did not appear to be much difference in the value of the different grades of wheat. Even the "Feed" sample proved by no means useless for bread-making purposes, either in yield or quality; the only thing that rendered it less available for bakers' use was its darker color. All who saw the loaves were surprised at the quality of this bread.

The tests on these 1903 samples confirmed the farmers in their opinion that on 1903 wheat the spread in price between No. 1 Hard and No. 4 was not in harmony with the milling quality. From No. 1 Hard the amount of flour obtained was 70.8 per cent. as against 68 per cent. from the No. 4 grade. The large percentage of stook-frozen grain that went into the lower grades because it was technically debarred from the higher ones no doubt raised the milling value, it was thought, of all the grades that year.

The Department of Agriculture for the Territories therefore decided to repeat the tests with 1904 wheat. The samples with which Professor Harcourt was furnished represented the grain just as it was sold by the farmer and graded either at the elevator or by the Chief Grain Inspector; it was not a composite sample of the commercial grades. The second tests practically confirmed the work done the previous year. The milling, chemical and baking tests failed to show very wide differences in the composition and milling value of the grades submitted. The conclusion reached was that the difference in composition and milling value was nearly as great between samples of any one grade as between the various grades.

The farmers began to feel that it would be a good thing to have a representative at Winnipeg to watch the grading of their cars and to look after their interests generally. The Department of Agriculture for the Territories was asked by the Sintaluta grain growers to appoint a man and W. H. Gaddes was commissioned to act for two weeks. Then the farmers began to wonder if they could not send down a man of their own; at one of their meetings the question was put and those present subscribed five dollars apiece for the purpose.

Thus it came about that on the 7th of January, 1905, there stepped from the train at the C. P. R. depot in Winnipeg a man who looked no different from any one of a dozen other farmers who daily reached the city, tanned of cheek and bright of eye. But his business in town was of a very special nature. In his pocket was a hundred dollars and the grip in his hand was packed for a month's stay.

It was a month of "cold shoulders" and patronizing manners for E. A. Partridge. No band music was played in his honor, no festive board was spread, nor was he taken around and shown the sights of the city. On the contrary, he was made to feel like a spy in the camp of an enemy; for he found himself entirely without status, the grain dealers recognizing him merely as a farmers' representative, whatever that was. Even at the office of the Chief Grain Inspector he was looked upon as a man who was meddling with something which he wasn't supposed to know anything about.

Nevertheless, the Chief Inspector himself gave him information at times and there were one or two others who took the trouble to explain some things about which he asked questions. Among the latter was a grain man by the name of Tom Coulter. For the most part, however, the presence of the "farmers' representative" at Winnipeg was looked upon as a joke; so that information as to the grain business became for him largely a still hunt. He visited offices, listened to how interviews were conducted over the telephone and picked up whatever loose ends he could find to follow up.

"Who is that fellow, anyway?" asked a grain man who had just got back to the city. He jerked his thumb over his shoulder.

"Oh, him!" laughed his partner as he saw who was indicated. "Only that gazabo from Sintaluta who's been nosing around lately. Some hayseeds out the line sent him down here to learn the grain business. They believe that all wheat's No. 1 Hard, all grain buyers are thieves, and that hell's to be divided equally between the railways and the milling companies!"

"So that's the guy, eh?—that's that man Partridge!"

[1] The new name of Rat Portage is Kenora (Ontario).

[2] See Appendix—Par. 2.

[3] See Appendix—Par. 8.

CHAPTER V

"THE HOUSE WITH THE CLOSED SHUTTERS"

Knock, knock, knock! Who's there, i' the name of Beelzebub? Here's a farmer. .

—Macbeth.

When wheat ceased to be grown for local needs and overflowed upon the markets of the world, becoming a factor in finance, arenas where its destiny was decided were established in the large centres of trade. In these basins of commerce the never-ending flow concentrated and wheeled for a short space before in re-directed currents it rolled on its way to ocean ports. Here, according to the novelists, frantic men were sucked into the golden eddies, their cries strangled and their fate forgotten even as they were engulfed by the Leviathan with which they adventured; or they emerged with eyes bloodshot, voices gone and clothes torn, successful speculators of a day. Perhaps the general reader is more familiar with these mad scenes of "The Pit," as the trading floor is called, than with the steadily turning marketing machinery of which they are but a penumbra.

The modern grain exchange is much more than a mere roulette wheel for the speculator. Its real purpose is to provide a centre for the legitimate trader. It is a great information bureau of world happenings where every item of news concerning the wheat in any way is gathered and classified—drouth, rain, frost, rust, locusts, hail, Hessian fly, monsoon or chinch bug. In every corner of the earth where the wheat streams take their rise, from green blade to brown head the progress of the crop is recorded and the prospects forecasted—on the steppes of Russia, the pampas of the Argentine, the valley of the San Joaquin, the prairies of Western Canada and the Dakotas, the fields of India, Iowa, Illinois and Kansas. Good news, bad news, the movements of ships, the prices on the corn exchanges of London and Liverpool, at Chicago, on the bourses of Paris, Antwerp and Amsterdam—all are listed. With such a Timepiece of International Exchange ticking out the doings of nations, both buyer and seller can know what prices will govern their dealings. In office or farmhouse an ear to a telephone is all that is necessary.

A grain exchange, then, is the market-place where grain dealers meet to secure information and maintain regulations for the prompt performance of contracts. The exchange organization does not deal in grain, but has for its sole purpose the protection of those who do and the facilitating of transactions; in other words, it is on the ground to see that the grain trade is carried on in an honest and capable manner and to punish offenders against proper business ethics and established rules.

Its membership is composed of grain dealers doing business in the exchange's territory—milling companies, exporting companies, line elevator companies as well as independent dealers and "commission men." Besides seeking a supply of wheat to keep their mills busy for the season, the milling companies sell wheat. It is the business of the exporters to make shipment to other countries. Wheat is sold to exporters and millers by the elevator companies, who are interested in running as much grain as possible through their elevators at country points. The chief business of independent dealers is to handle wheat that stands "on track," ready for shipment, either buying outright from the farmer or handling it for him on a commission basis.

The "commission man" is in an especially good position to do a clean-cut business. He assumes no burden of large capital investment and operating expense, as do the elevator companies. His chief need is a line of credit at a bank and from this he pays advances to his clients, his security being the bills of lading of wheat consigned to him. He does not need to buy or sell on his own account and, unlike the exporter, he does not have to risk changes in freight rates or in prices or make deliveries by given dates. As for the satisfactory milling quality of the crop—that is something for the miller to worry over. In order to do business it is necessary only for the commission man to be a member of the exchange and to obey its rules.

For a long time Winnipeg has been known as the greatest primary wheat market in the world. That means that a greater volume of new wheat, direct from the producer, passes through the Winnipeg market than anywhere else, not even excepting Chicago where the first grain exchange to reach international development was established in 1848. The Winnipeg market is fed by the vast wheat area of Western Canada and frequently between two and three million bushels of wheat go through Winnipeg in a single day. During the rush season sixty or seventy cars of wheat leave Winnipeg for the East every twenty minutes of every twenty-four hours. The freight boats on the lakes load 460,000 bushels in three-and-a-half hours.[1]

It is interesting to note that nowhere else in the world is a great public grain market like the Winnipeg market found located four hundred miles away from the storage point where grain dealt in is kept for sale delivery. Geographically Fort William and Port Arthur at the head of the great lakes water route would provide the natural delivery point for Western grain which has been routed eastward[2] and there the location of the exchange might be looked for logically. It so happens, however, that the eastern edge of the vast grain fields lies four hundred miles west of the twin harbors, the country between not being adapted for farming, and to avoid the delay of mail transit and to operate the trading effectively it was necessary to locate the exchange at Winnipeg, the great metropolitan railway centre where the incoming grain concentrated.

In Western Canada the grain is stored in bulk by grades, thereby cheapening handling cost. Unlike most countries— which sell grain on sample—Western Canadian grain has been sold by grade. The inspection and grading of wheat, therefore, is a very important factor in the grain trade of Canada and is in full charge of Dominion Government officials. Upon their verdict depends the price per bushel which will be paid for any shipment of grain, market quotations varying for different grades; whether stored, sold at home or sold abroad their certificate of grade brands that particular wheat throughout. The huge river of grain flows in upon them unceasingly; at times the inspectors have to work at top speed to avoid being engulfed. The variety of Nature's response to the growing conditions in changing seasons must not confuse them from year to year; but with sharpened senses and sound judgment they must steer a sure course through the multiplicity of grades and grade subdivisions.

The thoroughness of the system adopted by the Grain Inspection Department is shown by description of the work done at Winnipeg. Offices and staffs in charge of deputy inspectors are maintained in the different railway yards. They work in shifts night and day; for during the mad seventy-or-so days in which the Western crop stampedes for the lakefront there is no let-up to the in-rolling wheat-bins which come swaying and grinding in over the rails like beads on a string—the endless rosary of harvest thanksgiving. Wheat samples must be obtained from each car and no train can be moved until a placard has been placed at the end of it, reading: "Grain Inspectors have finished this train." A fifty-car train can be sampled in about an hour and a half, which is comfortable time for a change of engines and crews.

The sampling gangs work with all the precision of gun crews—each man with a particular thing to do. One goes down the train, opening car doors and leaving an empty sample bag in each car. Running up a short ladder, the sampler climbs over the top of the inner door, which extends above the "load line"; the standard sampler which he uses is a cylindrical brass rod, so constructed that when it is "stabbed" to the bottom of the car the grain which fills it is a correct sample of wheat at every depth. Seven such samples are procured from different sections of the car, and the track foreman, standing on a ladder, watches these poured onto a cloth with an eye to detecting evidence of "plugging" with an inferior quality of grain; these seven samples having been mixed thoroughly, a canvas bag is filled from the result and the two-and-one-half pounds which it will hold become the official sample. The rest of the mixture is dumped back and the car resealed.

The foreman has filled out a sample ticket with car number, date, load line, initials of sampler and any other notations necessary—such as leakages, etc. His own name is stamped on the back of the ticket, which goes into the sample sack. Copies of the way bills with full information as to all cars, shipping points, consignees or advisees and destinations are obtained from the railway yard office and these, together with the samples, are sent twice a day to the Chief Grain Inspector's office at the Grain Exchange.

Here the samples are inspected and graded in a room with special lighting facilities. The grading is done only in broad daylight. The quality of the grain, its condition and the admixtures are determined respectively by judgment of hand and eye, by elaborate mechanical moisture tests and by a sieving and weighing process. The whole sample is examined closely for color, plumpness, weight, etc., in order to fix its grade as No. 1 Hard, No. 1 Northern, 2 Northern, 3 Northern; 1 Hard and 1 Northern must weigh at least sixty pounds, 2 Northern fifty-eight pounds, and so on. Grades below these are set by the Grain Standards Board. Damp or wet grain is marked "No Grade," which means that it is considered unfit for storing and therefore has a lower market value. Grain which is heated or bin-burnt is "condemned." If it is unsound, musty, dirty, smutty, sprouted or badly mixed with other grain, etc., it is "rejected." Grain which, because of weather or other conditions, cannot be included in the grades provided by statute is given a "commercial grade."

It will be seen at once that here is work requiring great nicety of judgment and that long experience is necessary to enable the grader to reach his decisions quickly and accurately. When the grading is completed the sample is placed in a small tin box and filed systematically; it is supposed to remain thus stored until there is no longer the possibility of a demand for re-inspection and finally the samples are sacked and sold to the miller with the highest bid, the money being paid to the Dominion Government.

Grade certificates, bearing the Chief Grain Inspector's signature, are issued for each shipment and sent at once to the elevator company, miller or commission agent to whom the car is consigned. These grade certificates, together with the weight certificate and the bill of lading, make the grain negotiable on the market; the dealer does not see the actual grain, merely handling these papers.

If dissatisfaction with grade or dockage arises, the owner of the grain or his agent can obtain re-inspection at the office of the Chief Grain Inspector free of charge, and, if still dissatisfied, appeal can be made to the Survey Board. This is a board of twelve men; the governing rules and regulations are established by the Grain Commission. Six members are recommended by the Winnipeg Board of Trade and two each by the Minister of Agriculture in each of the three prairie provinces.[3] The verdict of the Survey Board is final.

Now, back in 1905 the machinery for moving the crop upon its way was little understood by the average Western Canadian farmer. The wheels went around, gave a click and away went his wheat; but in approaching it all with the idea of understanding everything he was in the position of the small boy examining the works of a watch to see how it told the time. He felt that he ought to understand what went on down at Winnipeg; for of course where there were so many rules and regulations to be broken there must be "funny work." It was the natural suspicion of the man who lived much to himself in the quiet spaces, who could not believe that grain dealers could be honest and build palatial residences in Winnipeg while his own toil in producing the grain was rewarded with a living only. It looked as if the roost was being robbed and with his newborn initiative he wanted to find out how it was done and who was doing it.

The satisfactory manner in which things are conducted in the grain trade to-day is the result of long experience and gradual improvement of conditions. It must be remembered that in the earlier days the trade was not so well organized for efficiency and in 1905 when E. A. Partridge began to probe for "plugging" he had a big job on his hands, especially in view of the fact that he was treated for the most part as a meddler who was not entitled to reliable information.

There are two ways of reaching a conclusion—one by approaching it logically on facts laid down; the other by jumping to it across a yawning lack of detail. At the end of his month of investigation the farmer's scout had a regular rag-bag of material out of which to fashion a patchwork report. A grain man might have condemned it as a "crazy quilt" because bits of high color obtruded inharmoniously. But if here and there an end was short or a bit of information on the bias, it was because the "Farmers' Representative" had not been treated with sufficient frankness. He had to make the best of the materials allowed him and his natural tendency to bright-colored metaphor may have been quickened. He hit out straight from the shoulder in all sincerity at conditions as they appeared to him.

He thought he saw five companies controlling the exporting business, and also their margin of profit, so that they were able to keep out smaller dealers who might have the temerity and the necessary capital to try exporting on their own account. He saw the smaller dealers in turn stem-winding their prices by those of the exporters, controlling the prices paid for street and track wheat throughout the country; thereby, he reasoned, it became possible to set special prices at any given point by the simple expedient of wiring the necessary instructions to the operator at that point to pinch independent competition. He saw elevator companies cutting their charges at certain points to kill off competition from "farmers' elevators" which sold to independent dealers. All this he was sure he saw.

The sampling appeared to be carried on in a systematic and

satisfactory manner. The grading, too, appeared to be uniform enough as regarded the standard grades; but in the item of color there seemed just cause for complaint. Lack of color, a trifling number of imperfectly formed kernels or the suspicion of a wrinkle on the bran apparently doomed a sample to low grade no matter how heavy and flinty the wheat might be.

This seemed scarcely fair to Partridge, who bore in mind that the sunny seasons of past years had been succeeded by cloudier ones, the dry autumns by wet ones and that with stacking discontinued and much of the farmers' wheat left long in stock, bleaching was bound to follow. So that if the Chief Grain Inspector were a "crank on color," he should remember that beauty was only skin deep.

The fracture and microscopic and weighing tests seemed to be the only reasonable tests which could be applied quickly; the milling test was the only one which was absolutely correct. Any rapid eye test which pretended to determine whether there was sixty-one per cent. or fifty-nine per cent. of Red Fife wheat in a given sample struck the Farmers' Representative as farcical; yet this was sufficient to make the difference of a grade and sometimes a difference of seven cents per bushel in the price obtained.

The whim of the Inspector likewise decided how many lean berries in a plump sample would disqualify it for "plump" classification and how many mature or defective berries among sound wheat, would disqualify it from being classed as "sound." With a single concocted sample as a basis of judgment Partridge considered that the grading of the lower grades often was very unjust to the producer, especially to the owners of plump frosted wheat; the process of concocting the basic sample was very interesting; but the result was "a nightmare."

W. H. Gaddes, who had preceded him to Winnipeg, agreed with him in this. Also, Mr. Gaddes denounced the Survey Board at that time as unsatisfactory in its composition, open to suspicion in its findings and in practice—so far as outsiders' wheat was concerned—simply a machine to register confirmation of the Inspector's previous grading.

It was Partridge's belief that "many a fraud perpetrated in a line elevator" was added to the "iniquities" of the Inspector, in whose personal integrity he had every confidence. For this reason he was inclined to be lenient with the hard-working and conscientious officials of the Government. Nevertheless, it appeared wise that a farmers' special agent be maintained permanently at Winnipeg to safeguard the interests of the farmers, especially if certain powers were allotted to him under the Inspection Act.

In making his report to the Territorial Grain Growers' Association Partridge went into the whole situation as he saw it and particularly was he outspoken in regard to "that House with the Closed Shutters," as he called the Winnipeg Grain and Produce Exchange. In fact, his gas attack upon the Exchange was ablaze with the fires of hostility.

And for the use of his reckless language Partridge was to be called to account in due course.

[1] Although only about ten per cent. of the arable area in Western Canada is under cultivation there are already 3,500 country elevators. Terminal elevators at the head of the lakes with a storage capacity of forty-four million bushels and interior Government terminals with ten and one-half million bushels capacity are overflowing already. Wheat exports of Canada have increased from 2,284,702 bushels in 1867 to 157,745,469 bushels in 1916. Per capita Canada has more railway mileage than any country in the world.

[2] In early days nearly all grain was routed eastward via Winnipeg; but with the development of the grain trade and the opening of the Panama Canal some Western Canadian grain travels west and south. Facilities for inspection and grading have been established at Calgary, Superior, Duluth, Saskatoon, Moose Jaw, Medicine Hat and Vancouver.

[3] In 1905 three members of the Survey Board were recommended by the Winnipeg Board of Trade and three each by the respective Departments of Agriculture in the three Prairie Provinces.

CHAPTER VI

ON A CARD IN THE WINDOW OF
WILSON'S OLD STORE

. . . Is it vain to hope
The sons of such a land will climb and grope
Along the undiscovered ways of life,
And neither seek nor be found shunning strife,
But ever, beckoned by a high ideal,
Press onward, upward, till they make it real;
With feet sure planted on their native sod,
And will and aspirations linked with God?

—Robert J. C. Stead.

Ideas grow. The particular idea which now began to occupy the thoughts of E. A. Partridge to the exclusion of everything else was a big idea to begin with; but it kept on growing so rapidly that it soon became an obsession.

Why couldn't the farmers themselves form a company to undertake the marketing of their own wheat? That was the idea. If a thousand farmers got together in control of ten million bushels of wheat and sold through a single accredited agency, they would be in the same position exactly as a single person who owned ten million bushels. If the owner of

Hopkins Moorhouse

ten thousand bushels was able to make a better bargain than the owner of one thousand, what about the owner of ten million bushels?

"Would the owner of ten million bushels peddle his wheat by the wagonload at the local shipping point or by the carload in Winnipeg?" mused Partridge. "Would he pay one hundred thousand dollars to a commission man to sell his wheat, with perhaps a nice rake-off to an exporter, who turns it over at a profit by selling it to a British dealer, who blends it and makes a good living by selling the blend to a British miller?"

His pencil travelled swiftly on the back of an envelope.

"Would he pay one hundred and seventy-five thousand dollars to the line elevator and stand a dockage of one hundred thousand bushels in addition? Would he pay the terminal elevator seventy-five thousand dollars' worth of screenings? Would he pay two and one-half million dollars for transportation when 'by a little method known to large exporters' he could save one and a quarter million dollars out of this item?

"You just bet he wouldn't!" concluded this man Partridge. "And supposing we had ten thousand farmers in one company and each farmer produced, on an average, five thousand bushels of wheat—that would put the company in control of the sale of *fifty* million bushels, not ten! Why, there's the answer to the whole blame thing—so simple we've been stepping right over it!"

Pools, mergers, combines, trusts and monopolies were but various forms of the same co-operative principle acting within narrow limits to the benefit of the co-operatives and the prejudices of the outsiders. The remedy lay not in legislative penalties against co-operation but in the practice of co-operation on a large scale by the people. That would provide the most powerful weapon of defence against financial buccaneering. Universally employed, it would bring about an industrial millennium!

But this was dreaming, of course. None knew better than E. A. Partridge that if even a small part of it was to come true, there lay immediately ahead a great educational campaign. Ignorance and suspicion would require to be routed. It would be difficult to convince some farmers that his motives were unselfish. Others would be opposed to the idea of a farmers' trading company in the belief that it would wreck the Association. "We must keep our organization non-partizan, non-political and non-trading" had been the slogan from the first.

Nothing daunted by the difficulties which loomed in the foreground, Partridge obtained permission from his Territorial associates to tell the central Manitoba Grain Growers' Association the result of his investigations at Winnipeg. The Manitoba convention was about to be held at Brandon and on his way back home he remained over to address the delegates. They listened carefully to what he had to say; but when he began to urge the necessity of the farmers themselves going into trading in grain his fire and enthusiasm caused more excitement where he was standing on the platform than in the audience. The best he could do by his earnestness was to create sufficient interest for a committee[1] to be appointed with instructions to investigate the possibilities of the scheme and report at the next annual convention of the Manitoba Grain Growers' Association.

On arrival at Sintaluta, however, he succeeded in stirring up his neighbors to the proper pitch of enthusiasm. They knew him at Sintaluta, listened to him seriously, and the leaders of the little community shook hands on the idea of organizing, in the form of a joint stock company, "a scheme for the co-operative marketing of grain by farmers."

When he made his report of the Winnipeg investigations at the annual convention of the Territorial Grain Growers' Association at Moose Jaw he found that while the principle which he advocated was favorably received—just as it had been in Manitoba—many farmers drew back distrustfully from the idea of "going into business." Their experience with business in the past had not been of a nature to instill confidence in such a venture and if the enterprise failed, they feared it would discredit the Association. There was a strong prejudice against any Association director or officer being closely identified with such a propaganda.

Back to Sintaluta went E. A. Partridge. A public meeting was called to discuss the situation. It was to be held in the Town Hall on January 27th (1906) and in preparation for it a preliminary meeting was held in the sitting-room of the hotel and a committee[2] appointed to prepare a synopsis of what was to be done.

This synopsis was presented to the thirty farmers who gathered in the Town Hall and a lengthy resolution was passed unanimously, setting forth the aims and objects of the prospective trading company. Everybody present undertook to subscribe for shares.

Justification for what they were attempting was found in "the widespread discontent existing among the grain growers of the West with conditions governing the marketing of their grain." It was pointed out also that the isolation of farmers from each other, their distance from the secondary and ultimate markets and their ignorance of the details of the grain business—that these things rendered them individually liable to suffer grave injustices, even without their knowledge and certainly without hope of remedy by individual efforts. The scientific selling of wheat was just as important to the farmer as the scientific growing of it and this scientific knowledge could be obtained only by actually engaging in the business at some important commercial centre where the methods of successful operators could be studied.

There was every reason to believe that a scheme which limited its activities at first to acquiring a seat on the Grain Exchange and doing a straight commission business, or at most a commission and track-buying business—that such a co-operative scheme stood an excellent chance of success. Without much financial risk, it should prove immediately profitable, afford protection from crooked practices and at the same time the shareholders could gain an insight into the whole grain business and thereby equip themselves for greater enterprises; it would not be long before they would be in a position to deal intelligently with their problems and pertaining legislation. Besides all this there was the possible piling up of a surplus revenue, over and above dividends, which could be turned to good account in uncovering conditions in Eastern Canadian and European markets and learning the best ways to meet those conditions.

For these reasons the grain growers of Sintaluta, Saskatchewan, went on record at this meeting in the little Town Hall as heartily recommending the formation of a joint stock company which was to be composed wholly of farmers and to be known as "The Grain Growers' Grain Company, Limited," with shares at twenty-five dollars each. It was stipulated that no one person could hold more than four shares, that even these were not to be transferable except by vote at annual meeting, and that no man could have more than one vote at annual meetings. With this single far-sighted stroke the possibility of control passing into the hands of any clique was removed.

In furtherance of the plans set forth a committee[3] was named to take charge of the preliminary organization work until relieved by the election of a provisional directorate at an organization meeting which it was hoped to hold at Brandon the following March. This committee was authorized to conduct a campaign for subscriptions in the meantime, printed receipts to be issued for the same.

Such was the scheme to which the farmers of Sintaluta subscribed to a man. Two hundred shares at Sintaluta to begin with and Sintaluta only one point in the West! The Committee went to work with enthusiasm. Ten dollars was spent in printing a prospectus. E. A. Partridge got a card and blocked out on it: GRAIN GROWERS' GRAIN COMPANY. This he hung in the window of Wilson's old store at Sintaluta, where a dollar was paid for the use of a desk. Here in the evenings would assemble William Hall, Al Quigley, William Bonner and E. A. Partridge to send out circulars and keep the pot boiling till enough funds were on hand to let Quigley out canvassing on board wages.

On February 28th the Manitoba Grain Growers' Association held their 1906 convention and as chairman of the committee appointed the year before to report upon the matter, E. A. Partridge again urged the advisability of establishing a company to handle the farmers' grain. By this time the plan had taken more definite shape and he pressed the claims of the proposed commission company with such logic and eloquence that besides having the committee's report adopted by the Association unanimously, he secured the interest of quite a few delegates. There was, nevertheless, much adverse criticism, not a little apathy and some levity.

"Let's hold a meeting of our own," suggested someone. The

word was passed for all who were interested to meet in the council chamber of the Brandon Town Hall. Between twenty and thirty farmers attended this meeting and the plans of the Sintaluta men for a co-operative trading company were approved. It was decided to meet at the Leland Hotel in Winnipeg some time in March or April to formulate plans for an active campaign.

For two days those in attendance at this second meeting discussed the details of the undertaking. A great many different views were expressed, not all of them favorable. There were those who objected to the chosen name of the prospective company as being a handicap upon the Association movement in case the venture failed. The Sintaluta provisional directorate was allowed to stand and the canvassing committee was enlarged to include a number of Manitoba men who were to take the field for a stock canvass.

That stock-selling campaign will dodder through to the Final Memory of those who took part in it. The man who stood on the street-corner and offered ten-dollar gold-pieces for a dollar had no harder task. Blood from stones! Milk from dry cows! Although ten per cent. on each share was all the cash that was asked apparently some farmers were so hard up that if yarn were selling at five cents per mile, they couldn't buy enough of it to make a pair of mitts for a doodlebug!

"If you take four shares," admitted Al Quigley at his meetings, "I can't guarantee that you're not losing four times $2.50, which is ten dollars. But you lose that much when you draw a load of wheat up to the elevator anyway," he argued. "You might just as well let another ten go to see what's become of the first ten!"

"Huh!" grunted a skeptical farmer after one of E. A. Partridge's meetings. "This here thing's just a scheme for

Partridge to feather his nest! You bet he didn't get any o' my money," he bragged. "Did he get you, Pete?"

"He did, Ben, an' I'll tell you why. This thing'll probably go bust; but I put a hundred into it. Supposin' I put a hundred in a horse an' he dies on me. Same thing, ain't it? I got to have horses to do farmin' an' I just go an' buy another one. I figure it's worth takin' a hundred-dollar chance on this thing to try her out."

Up in the northern part of Manitoba was one man who was meeting with pretty fair success. His name was Kennedy and his friends who knew him best called him "Honest John." His plan was simple—to start talking, talk for awhile, then keep right on talking.

"For God's sake, Kennedy, if $2.50 will stop you talking, here it is! We're sleepy!"

Then he would stop talking.

One by one the original canvassers dropped out of the field till almost the only one left besides E. A. Partridge was this hard-talking enthusiast up in the Swan River country who wound himself up for the night and tired them out—but got the money!

[1] See Appendix—Par. 4.

[2] See Appendix—Par. 5.

[3] See Appendix—Par. 6.

CHAPTER VII

A FIGHT FOR LIFE!

My dear little Demus! you'll find it is true,
He behaves like a wretch and a villain to you . . .

—Aristophanes.

It was characteristic of John Kennedy to keep everlastingly at it. He was used to hard things to do. In this life some men seem to get rather more than their share of tacks in the boots and crumbs in bed! But every time Fate knocked him down he just picked himself up again. Always he got up and went at it once more—patiently, conscientiously, smiling. Even Fate cannot beat a man like that and John Kennedy was a hard fighter in a quiet way who did not know how to quit.

With four younger brothers and an equal number of younger sisters to crowd up to the home table down there on the farm near Beaverton, Ontario County, Ontario, it was advisable for the eldest son to work out as a farm boy. He was thirteen years old when he first hired out to a farmer for the summer and he was to receive twenty-four dollars for the season. But the farmer had a hard time that year and at the end of the summer—

"John," said the poor fellow with ill-concealed embarrassment, "I—I'm afraid I can't pay you that money. But you know that big flock of sheep down in the back pasture? Well, tell you what we'll do. Over at Beaverton I've got an uncle who's a tailor. I can give you a suit of full cloth of homespun and call it square," and though the boy wanted the money for fifty things he had to take the homespun suit.

Three or four hobble-de-hoy years of it on the farms of the neighborhood and young Kennedy literally took to the woods and drove the rivers in Muskoka and Michigan as a lumberjack till he was a chunk of whalebone in a red flannel shirt and corked boots and could pull the whiskers out of a wild-cat! With varying success he fought the battle of life and learned that many things glitter besides gold and that the four-leafed clover in this life after all is a square deal between men.

The appeal of E. A. Partridge at the convention of the Manitoba Grain Growers in 1906 therefore found John Kennedy feeling responsive. He knew the unjust position in which the farmers were placed; for he was a farmer himself—up in the Swan River Valley—and he was a delegate from the Swan River Grain Growers' Association. The idea of forming a farmers' commission company for handling the farmers' grain sounded like a very satisfactory solution of a very unsatisfactory state of affairs and he threw himself whole-heartedly into the campaign to sell enough stock to obtain a charter.

Up in the newer part of the country, which was his own particular territory, he found the farmers ready enough to listen; for they had suffered up there from the evils at which the new movement was aiming. He found also that the most interested members of his audiences were men who could least afford to lose any money.

An effort was made to discredit the whole proposition as a political move of the Conservative Party. Throughout the Swan River district, the Dauphin district and all the way down to Neepawa the rumor spread ahead of the meetings; so that the speakers were asked many pertinent and impertinent questions, J. W. Robson, a Swan River farmer who was at that time a Conservative Member of the Manitoba Legislature, was giving his services free as a speaker on behalf of the proposed company; John Kennedy was known to be a political supporter of J. W. Robson. One and one make two; two and two sometimes make a fairly large-sized political rumor. But Mr. Robson was a ready and convincing speaker who was known to be a farmer first and last and Mr. Kennedy attributes the practical results obtained as due largely to Mr. Robson's logic and sincerity.

Along in June Kennedy received a telegram from Winnipeg that startled him. It contained the first intimation that difficulties were arising at Ottawa to prevent the proposed farmers' company from getting their charter. Taking the first train, he found on his arrival at Winnipeg that Francis Graham and W. A. Robinson, the two committeemen who met him, had not yet notified E. A. Partridge. A wire was despatched at once to Sintaluta and the Chairman joined them by first train. For two days the Board wrestled with this unexpected difficulty which threatened to annihilate the company before it got started.

The application of the Organization Committee for a charter was refused on the ground that the shares of a company with a capital of $250,000 could not be less than $100 each. Their solicitor tried in vain to induce the Department to change its views, all canvassing to sell stock being discontinued by the Committee in the meantime.

"Well, let 'em keep their charter if they want to," said

Kennedy finally. "This discussion's not getting us anywhere and if we can't get a Dominion charter, why we can't get it."

"Guess you're right, John. We might as well quit and go on home."

"Who said anything about quitting?" Kennedy brought down his big fist on the table with a thump. "We'll get a Manitoba charter. That's what I mean."

The others shook their heads. A Provincial charter would be useless for what they were proposing to do, they contended. Kennedy disagreed so emphatically that he refused to stop arguing about it till at last he and John Spencer were delegated to see the Manitoba authorities. In the course of a few days the arrangements for a Provincial charter were complete, and the Committee turned its attention to selling enough stock to be ready for business by the middle of the following month.

By this time the harvest season was so near at hand that prompt action was necessary if they were to do any business that fall. Under the Manitoba charter the company could open for business with a provisional directorate and as five members of the original committee were in Winnipeg and available for quick action, it was decided to go ahead as it would be impossible to hold a representative general meeting of the shareholders before harvest and it was advisable in the interests of the subscribers to take advantage of the opportunity to do business in the meantime.

Provisional organization therefore was undertaken during the week of the Winnipeg Industrial Exhibition, in a tent on the Fair grounds, and July 26th was set as the date. When space was sought for the erection of their sixteen-foot tent, however, they found themselves classed with the "Sunflower

Belles" and "Katzenjammer Castle" and it was only after the payment of fifty dollars that permission was granted for the erection of the tent. Here to the accompaniment of a raucous medley of sounds—the beating of tom-toms, the ballyhooing of the sideshows, the racket of the machinery exhibits and the cries of the peanut and lemonade vendors—the farmers' trading company was organized with provisional officers[1] and directorate in legal shape to start the wheels in motion as a joint stock company.

But before actual business could begin a manager must be located who knew all the ins and outs and ups and downs of the grain business; also a seat upon the Winnipeg Grain Exchange must be purchased before the farmers could enter the arena as dealers in grain. None of the officers of the young company which was about to try its wings overlooked the fact that nothing could be more foolhardy than for farmers like themselves, direct from the green pastures, to attempt the plunge they were about to take without proper guidance as to the depth of the water and the set of the currents. They knew they were embarking in a most intricate and difficult business and with so much at stake on behalf of the whole farming population of Western Canada it was necessary to place the helm in the hands of somebody who could pilot them through the shoals. At best it promised to be a stormy passage.

About the only man in sight for the position was Thomas Coulter, of the Independent Grain Company. He had treated E. A. Partridge with more consideration as the "Farmers' Representative" than most of the other grain men and there was a possibility that he might be persuaded to take the offer seriously. But on approaching him, Mr. Coulter did not become excited over the prospect of managing a farmers' company in the grain business; even he was not inclined to take too seriously the effort of the farmers to do their own trading. How long would the farmers stand behind the company in the face of the competition that would be brought to bear? That was the question that bulged right out in front; for, as everybody knew, farmers never had been able to hang together very long when it came down to a matter of dollars and cents in their individual pockets. Finally, however, he agreed that there might be a fighting chance and accepted the management.

So far so good. But what about the seat on the Grain Exchange? The price of it was $2,500. One thousand shares of the company's stock had been disposed of with ten per cent. paid up and from the $2,500 thus realized the expenses of organization had to be met, the charter paid for, the legal fee and expenses at Ottawa in connection with the effort to secure a Dominion charter, office rent, printing bills and what not.

"Which leaves us about $1,000 to buy a $2,500 seat and finance our first business operations," said John Spencer with the look of a worried Secretary-Treasurer.

"We'll have to issue a twenty per cent. call on subscribed stock," admitted the President reluctantly. "In the meantime I'll have to see if some of the boys out at Sintaluta will go security for the fifteen hundred. Thank heaven, these fellows down here think we're a hilarious joke! The only chance we've got to get through the fence with this thing is for them to keep right on laughing at us till we get our toes in the sand!"

He wrote to Sintaluta, explaining the situation, and five of E. A. Partridge's friends[2] at once responded by going to the bank with their personal notes for the amount needed.

"With support like that we're going to win, boys," cried the

President proudly when the bank notified them that the money was available.

Financial arrangements were established with the Bank of British North America and when a room had been rented on the top floor of the old Tribune building and circulars sent broadcast among the farmers, soliciting grain, the wheels began to turn.

The little office was opened for business on September 5th (1906). It was so small that even two or three people got in each other's way, though all they were doing was to watch the mails anxiously for the first indications as to whether the farmers would stand behind the big idea that was now put to the test. Then came the bill of lading for the first carload of grain consigned to the new company, followed quickly by the second, the third, fourth, fifth, sixth—two at a time, three, ten, fifteen per day! Every foot of space in the little office was a busy spot and the lone typewriter clickety-clacked on the second-hand table with cheerful disregard of lunch hours. By the end of the month the weekly receipts had risen to one hundred cars of grain.

It became necessary to move to a larger office and accommodation was obtained in the Henderson Block. At the present rate, a whole floor would be needed soon.

Over at the Grain Exchange some men were talking seriously. They were talking about E. A. Partridge and they were not laughing. The Secretary of the Exchange was instructed to write a letter.

Partridge hit the desk so hard that the paper-knife with which he had sliced open that letter hopped to the floor.

"They're after us already!" he exploded.

It looked that way. The Company's seat on the Grain Exchange was held in the name of the President and the letter summoned him to appear before the Council of the Exchange to answer to a charge of having sinned against the honor and "diginity" of that institution and of violating its rules. A short time before the young company had issued a circular setting forth their intention of dividing co-operatively whatever profits were earned; in other words, the man sending the larger amount of grain would receive the larger profits. This, the Exchange claimed, was a violation of the strict rules of the Grain Exchange and would have to be abandoned.

"You are virtually splitting the commission with the shipper," claimed the Exchange, "and we can't allow that for a minute."

"It's up to you to prove I'm guilty, not up to me to come here and commit myself," argued Partridge. "If you can find any profits that have been distributed co-operatively by the Grain Growers' Grain Company, go ahead. Nor have I sinned against your 'diginity'!" he added, sarcastically taking advantage of the stenographer's error in spelling. "For that matter, you've been digging into me ever since I came on here!"

"You can't do any more business with our members till you change your ways," declared the Exchange and forthwith, on October 25th, notice was posted to all Exchange members that any of them found dealing with the farmers' company would be penalized themselves.

Expelled from trading privileges! Practically boycotted! It was a straight punch on the nose that threatened to put the young organization out of business for the final count. Membership in the Exchange was absolutely imperative if the farmers were to be in a position to sell grain to exporters;

they were not strong enough yet to export direct to Old Country markets and all the exporters through whom they were compelled to deal were members of the Exchange.

"The whole thing's just a pretext!" cried Partridge vehemently. "We haven't got any by-law regarding distribution of profits co-operatively; the only thing they've got to go on is that circular. They're beginning to get scared of us and they see a chance to put us out of business."

If this were the object, it looked as if it might be achieved in short order. The grain was pouring in steadily by the carload and with no buyer daring to deal with them in face of the mandate from the Exchange, of which they were all members, the new company was in a quandary to dispose of the incoming grain on a falling market. The only thing they could do was to wait until they had sufficient of any grade to make a shipment of from 8,000 to 10,000 bushels of that grade and try to place it somewhere in the East. The Manager was sent east hurriedly to see what connections he could establish while his office assistant mailed letter after letter to eastern points in an endeavor to work several contracts.

The farmers who shipped their grain to the new company were expecting to receive seventy-five per cent. of an advance from the bank on their bills of lading and a prompt remittance of the balance when the Inspection Certificate and Outturn were in the hands of the Company. With the grain piling up on their company day by day, it was not long before the overdraft at the bank began to assume alarming proportions.

Luckily the Assistant Manager succeeded in making several sales in the East, which eased away from the crisis which was shaping. It was quite patent that it would have been suicide for the young trading organization to notify the farmers to stop sending in business. They dare not do that.

In desperation the President and Vice-President went to the Manitoba Government and laid their case in full before the cabinet. Premier R. P. Roblin (now Sir Rodmond Roblin) was very much surprised to learn the facts.

"The Government certainly cannot countenance any such action on the part of the grain dealers," he declared emphatically. "We cannot allow them to boycott a company composed of farmers who have as much right to sell grain as any other body of men."

Accordingly the Government set a time limit within which the Exchange had the option of removing the ban against the farmers' company or of losing their Provincial charter. In the meantime, however, this did not obtain restoration of trading privileges, without which the farmers' company could not do business with Exchange members except by paying them the full commission of one cent per bushel.

The situation, therefore, was approaching a crisis rapidly. The company was fortunate in having the friendship of their local bank manager; but even he could not go on forever making advances on consigned grain and there was some suspicion that letters were reaching the head office of the bank in Montreal, advising that the quicker this particular account was closed out the better off the bank would be.

Then one morning the local manager called on the Executive and his face was grave.

"This is not the first time I've heard from the Head Office about this account, as you know," he began at once, "but I'm afraid it's the last call, gentlemen." He handed a letter to the

President. "As you see, I am instructed to close out your account at once unless further security is forthcoming. I'm sorry; for I believe you've merely run into hard luck in getting squared away. But—I'm not the bank, you understand."

"What do you want us to do? What can we do?" asked Partridge anxiously. "This thing will straighten out, Mr. Machaffie. We're getting the business. You know that. We're going to get back our trading privileges and everything will be alright."

The banker shook his head slowly.

"I'm sorry, gentlemen. But do you know what your overdraft amounts to now?"

"Three hundred and fifty-six thousand dollars," murmured the Secretary-Treasurer.

"Exactly."

"What are we to do?"

"Before coming here I've been to see the Scottish Co-Operative Wholesale Society about taking some of your wheat. Fisher is ready to help you out if he finds he's not overstepping the rules of the Exchange. I may be able to carry you along for a short time if you three gentlemen, the Executive of your company, will give the bank your personal bond without limit as to the amount. I have even gone so far as to draw up the document for signature, if it meets with your approval."

"What about that, Kennedy? Spencer?"

"Guess we've got to do it," nodded Kennedy.

"Looks like it," agreed Spencer.

"Then—down she goes!" decided Partridge, dipping his pen in the ink. The others signed after him.

"That means we three go down with the ship," he remarked quietly after the door had closed upon the bank manager. "I appreciate you two fellows signing that thing." He got up and shook hands with each of them in turn. "If bad gets worse and we go to smash—"

"It can't get worse and we're not going to smash," reassured the others.

But that remained to be seen. Although placing grain in the East was robbing them of profits, it was the best that could be done to tide things over. The three active officials were on the anxious seat from morning till night. It had got down now to a question of meeting each day's events as they came and frequently the lights blazed in the little office till two and three in the morning while the provisional officers raked the situation from every angle in an endeavor to forecast the next day's difficulties and to prepare for them.

For three months the overdraft at the bank had averaged $275,000, due almost entirely to the conditions resulting from the action of the Exchange. It was useless to worry over the amount of interest which this accommodation was costing and the profits which might have been rolled up had things been different; the real worry was to keep going at any cost. For, as the bank manager had intimated, the whole thing was just hard luck rather than any unsoundness in the business. It was a fine paradox that the more pronounced the success of the idea itself became, the greater grew the danger of complete failure because of the predicament! Death by wheat! An ironical fate indeed for a grain company!

Upon investigation, the farmers' company discovered that their original idea of distributing their profits co-operatively—as embodied in the circular to which the Exchange had objected—was contrary to the provisions of the Manitoba Joint Stock Companies' Act under which they held their charter. Therefore the co-operative idea in connection with profits was formally dropped by the Grain Growers' Grain Company. This had been done at a directors' meeting on December 22nd (1906), when a resolution had been passed, cancelling the proposal contained in the objectionable circular.[3] But although the Exchange had been notified immediately and repeated applications for reinstatement had been made, the farmers' company was still struggling along in the throes of their dilemma—proof positive, concluded the farmers, that the Grain Exchange had used the co-operative suggestion as a mere pretext to oust the Company from the field altogether.

In piled the wheat, car after car of it! A considerable portion of it had been bought on track and farmers who had consigned their grain were anxious, naturally, to have it disposed of without delay. With prices going down and navigation on the point of closing, the best hopes of the management became centred in getting a big shipment away to Buffalo by boat. That would enable them to escape a big item in storage charges and to place the grain in line for export at rates considerably below the all-rail figures.

"With those bills of lading in the bank, we've no control of them and the bank can do just about as it likes," reviewed the President one night. "If they should come down on us to sell our wheat inside of forty-eight hours—we're goners, boys! All that those fellows over at the Exchange have got to do is to shove down the market thirty points and our name is *mud*! The loss to the farmers who've shipped us their grain will kill this movement and every one like it in the West for all time to come. This company will be as dead as a doornail and so will we financially as its bonded backers."

Kennedy was running a finger tentatively down the window-pane. It left a streak in the forming frost.

"What I want to know is, how long ought it to take to load up this whole boatload we're trying to move?"

"Oh, about seventeen hours or so."

"And how long have they been at it already? Five days, ain't it? And she's not away yet! What d'you suppose that means?" he snapped. He began to throw things into a grip. He made for the door.

"Where'n the mischief are you going, John?"

"Fort William—can just make the train if I hustle. The *J. P. Walsh* gets out of that harbor with that wheat of ours, by Hickory!—if she has to be chopped out with an axe!"

Two days later a telegram reached the little office:

S.S. J. P. Walsh cleared to-day for Buffalo. Three hundred and ten thousand bushels. Last boat out. KENNEDY.

[1] See Appendix—Par. 7.

[2] See Appendix—Par. 8.

[3] This resolution was confirmed at a meeting of the shareholders, February 5th, 1907.

CHAPTER VIII

A KNOCK ON THE DOOR

Every man is worth just as much as the things are worth about which he is concerned.

—*Marcus Aurelius.*

That big shipment to Buffalo, along with several others which were placed in the East with the market recovering, relieved the situation greatly. Also, the Scottish Co-Operative Wholesale Society's Winnipeg office decided to stand by the farmers' co-operative marketing venture and risked disapproval to buy some of the young company's wheat; not only that, but the farmers' company was allowed the regular commission of one cent per bushel on the purchase and the cheque paid in to the bank amounted to $58,298. This friendly co-operation the farmers were not quick to forget and they still speak of it with gratitude.

It began to look as if the struggling farmers' agency might worry through the winter after all. The strain of the past few months had told upon the men at the head of the young organization and especially upon the provisional President, who felt keenly the responsibilities of his office. Of a sensitive, high-strung temperament, E. A. Partridge suffered reaction to such a degree that at times he became almost despondent.

He began to talk of resigning. He felt that he had done quite a lot in getting things under way and that the hard fight which the farmers would have to wage before the trading company was established permanently would be carried on more successfully by a younger man. So frequently had his motives been questioned by suspicious farmers at organization meetings that he thought it would be better for the company if he occupied a less prominent place in the conduct of its affairs. The idea seemed to be prevalent that the organizers were enthusiastic for direct financial reasons. "Those fellows are talking for what they are going to get out of it," was an open accusation at times—a misconception so unjust that on several occasions Partridge had refuted it by pledging to resign from the presidency as soon as the company was on its feet.

"You men keep saying how much I've got out of this," he reproved in disheartened tones. "Gentlemen, I'll admit that I've got a little silver out of this. But it isn't in my pocket; it's in my hair!"

Partridge had no respect for a "quitter," however. He did not propose to take it easy until the farmers' agency did get into proper running order. Although his associates tried to dissuade him altogether from the course he had planned, the best he would promise was to remain at his post until the first annual meeting.

Immediately preceding the annual convention of the Manitoba Grain Growers' Association at Brandon in February a general meeting of Grain Growers' Grain Company shareholders was held with about two hundred represented. Until now the company had been operating under a provisional directorate only and it was the purpose of the meeting to complete organization. Since opening for business the shareholders had practically doubled in number and over 1,500,000 bushels of farmers' grain had been handled by their own agency, its ability to dispose of wheat at good figures being demonstrated in spite of deprivation of trading privileges on the Exchange. Putting a conservative estimate upon the holdings of the farmers' venture into co-operative marketing, its paid-up capital remained intact, its organization expenses paid—including the membership on the Grain Exchange—and there still was left a respectable margin of profit. To this showing the shareholders responded by electing the provisional directorate as directors for the balance of the year, adding two[1] to their number, while the same officers were left in charge.

In connection with the directorate it was pointed out that it might be better to have the trading company's directorate independent of the Association's directorate. The suggestion came from a tall young man who had a habit of thinking before he spoke and it was but one of many practical ideas which he had thrown out at the meeting.

"That young chap, Crerar, of Russell—makings of an able man there, Ed," commented the re-elected Vice-president later. "Know anything about him?"

"I know his father better than I do him," nodded the President thoughtfully. "I met his father in the old Patron movement years ago. I've got a great respect for his attitude of mind towards moral and economic questions. I like that young man's views, Kennedy; he seems to have a grasp of what this movement could accomplish—of the aims that might be served beyond the commercial side of it. In short, he seems to be somewhat of a student of economics and he has the education—used to be a school-teacher, I believe."

"Remember when I went up to Russell, during their Fair in October, to tell them what the Exchange was trying to do to us? Well, he was at the meeting and came over to my room at the hotel afterward," remarked Kennedy. "That's how interested he was. We had quite a talk over the whole situation. Told me he had an arrangement to buy grain for Graves & Reilly, besides running the Farmers' Elevator at Russell, and he offered to ship us all the grain that wasn't consigned to his firm. We've got quite a few carloads from him during the season."

"If there were only a few more elevator operators like him!" sighed Partridge. "When I was up there last July, selling stock, only eight men turned out," he recalled. "Crerar was one of them. I sold four shares. Crerar bought one. Say, he'd be a good man to have on the next directorate. How would it be if I wrote him a letter about it?"

But "Alex." Crerar laid that letter aside and promptly forgot it; he did not take it seriously enough to answer it. If there was anything he could do to help along a thing in which he believed as thoroughly as he believed in the grain growers' movement and the farmers' agency he was more than willing to do it; but executive offices, he felt, were for older and more experienced men than he.

As manager of an elevator in his home town, as buyer for a grain firm and as a farmer himself he had had opportunities for studying the situation from many angles. From the first he had followed the organization of the farmers with much interest and sympathy. He could not forget his own early experiences in marketing grain when the elevators offered him fifty-nine cents per bushel, nineteen cents under the price at the terminal at the time. The freight rate on his No. 1 Northern wheat he knew to be only nine cents per bushel and when he was docked a bushel and a half to a load of fifty bushels on top of it all he had been aroused to protest.

A protest from young Crerar was no mild and bashful affair, either. It was big-fisted with vigor. But when, with characteristic spirit, he had pointed out the injustice of the price offered and the dockage taken—the elevator man, quite calmly, had told him to go to the devil!

"There's no use going to the other elevators, for you're all alike," said young Crerar hotly.

"Then take your damned grain home again!" grinned the elevator operator insolently.

So the young farmer was compelled to sell his first wheat for what he could get. He was prepared to pay three cents per bushel on the spread, that being a reasonable charge; but although plenty of cars were available at the time, the spread cost him ten cents, a direct loss of seven cents per bushel. Besides this he was forced to see between twenty-five and thirty bushels out of every thousand appropriated for dockage, no matter how clean the wheat might be. That was in 1902.

It was hard to forget that kind of treatment. And when, later on, young Crerar accepted an offer of $75 per month to manage a Farmers' Elevator at Russell he bore his own experience in mind and extended every possible consideration to the farmers who came to him. The elevator company, as a company, did not buy grain; but as representative of Graves & Reilly, a Winnipeg firm, he bought odd lots and for this service received an extra fifty dollars per month.

Financially, it was better than teaching school. He had made ten dollars the first summer he taught school and to earn it he had walked three miles and a half each morning after milking the cows at home, arriving at the school soaking wet with dew from wading in the long prairie grass. And even at that, the trustees had wanted a "cheaper" teacher! A woman, they thought, might do it cheaper.

The young schoolmaster objected so earnestly, however, that the argument was dropped. He needed this money to assist in a plan for attending the Collegiate at Portage la Prairie. He taught the school so well that after studying Latin at Manitoba College in 1899, the trustees were glad to get him back the following year at a salary of $35 per month.

But milking cows at home night and morning and teaching school in between was not an exciting life at best for a young fellow ambitious to go farming. So at last he acquired a quarter-section of Hudson Bay Company land near Russell and took to "baching it" in a little frame shack.

In the fall some lumber was required for buildings and it so happened that along came an old chap with a proposition to put in a portable sawmill on a timber limit up in the Riding Mountains nearby. The old man meant business alright; he had the engine within ten miles of its destination before he was overtaken and the whole machine seized for debt. It looked as if the thousands of logs which the residents of the district had taken out for the expected mill had been piled up to no purpose. Crerar, however, succeeded in making a deal for the engine and, with a couple of partners, began sawing up logs. The little sawmill proved so useful that he ran it for four winters. When finally it was burned down no attempt was made to rebuild. Its owner was entering wider fields of activity.

After meeting Partridge and Kennedy his interest in the affairs of the farmers' little trading concern was quickened.

He was much impressed with the fact that here were men so devoted to an idea—so profound in their belief that it was the right idea—that its advancement was their first and only thought at all times. Alex. Crerar liked that. If a thing were worth attempting at all, it was worth every concentration of effort. What these men were trying to accomplish appealed to him as a big thing, a bigger thing than most of the farmers yet realized, and it deserved all the help he could give it. The little agency was in the thick of a fight against tremendous odds and that, too, had its appeal; for to a natural born fighter the odds meant merely a bigger fight, a bigger triumph.

Accordingly, the young man lost no opportunity to boost things along. He was able to consign many carloads of grain in a season. If an idea occurred to him that he thought might be of service he sat down and wrote a letter, offering the suggestion on the chance that it might prove useful to the Executive. He did everything he could to build up the Company's business in the Russell district and when he returned home from the shareholders' organization meeting he kept right on sending in business, offering helpful suggestions and saying a good word when possible.

As the weeks went by and it became more apparent that they would wind up their first year's business satisfactorily, E. A. Partridge decided definitely that he would not accept another term as President. There were several good men available to succeed him; but he could not get it out of his head that the one man for the tasks ahead was the young fellow up at Russell. When he went there in June to speak at a Grain Growers' picnic he drew Crerar aside for an hour's chat, found out why he had not answered the letter suggesting that he play a more active part, and liked him all the better for his modesty.

Without saying anything of what he had in mind he returned

to Winnipeg and sent the Vice-President to Russell to size up the situation quietly. When Kennedy got back he agreed with the President's choice of a successor.

The Company was holding its first annual meeting on July 16th and care was taken that the unsuspecting Crerar was on hand. The Vice-president button-holed him, explaining that he was wanted on the Board of Directors and in spite of his protest the President himself nominated him and he was elected promptly.

But when at the directors' meeting that night the President told the Board that he had been looking around for a young man to take charge and that T. A. Crerar was the man—when everybody present nodded approval, the man from Russell was speechless. If they had asked him to pack his grip and leave at once for Japan to interview the Mikado, he could not have been more completely surprised.

"Why, gentlemen" he objected, "I don't know anything about managing this company! I could not undertake it."

"What is the next order of business?" asked E. A. Partridge.

The shareholders were almost as much surprised as the newcomer himself when the name of the new president was announced. Many of them had never heard of T. A. Crerar. Had the young president-elect been able to see what lay ahead of him—

But, fortunately or unfortunately, that is one thing which is denied to every human being.

[1] See Appendix—Par. 7.

CHAPTER IX

THE GRAIN EXCHANGE AGAIN

"How many tables, Janet, are there in the Law?"

"Indeed, sir, I canna just be certain; but I think there's ane in the foreroom, ane in the back room an' anither upstairs."

—Scotch Wit and Humor (Howe).

The efforts of the elevator faction of the Winnipeg Grain and Produce Exchange, apparently to choke to death the Grain Growers' Grain Company, had awakened the farmers of the West to a fuller realization of the trading company's importance to the whole farmers' movement. The Grain Growers of the three prairie provinces had been watching things closely and they did not propose to let matters take their course unchallenged. A second Royal Commission had been appointed by the Dominion Government in 1906, under the chairmanship of John Millar, Indian Head, Saskatchewan, to probe conditions in the grain trade and the farmers felt that certain evidence which had been taken by this Commission at Winnipeg justified their claims that they were the victims of a combine.

In the latter part of November (1906) the President of the

Manitoba Grain Growers' Association, D. W. McCuaig, laid formal charges against three members of the Winnipeg Grain and Produce Exchange—charges of conspiring in restraint of trade—and when these gentlemen appeared in the Police Court it was evident that the Exchange intended to fight the case every inch of the way. The farmers discovered that the legal talent of Winnipeg had been cornered; for of the twenty lawyers to whom their solicitor, R. A. Bonnar, K.C., could turn for assistance in the prosecution every one appeared to have been retained by the defendants. The case involved such wide investigation that such assistance was imperative and finally the Grain Growers secured the services of ex-Premier F. W. G. Haultain,[1] of Saskatchewan.

The preliminary hearing in the Police Court proved to be most interesting and at times developed considerable heat among the battling legal lights. The defendants and their friends were so confident that commitment for trial would not be forthcoming at all that when the Magistrate decided that he was justified in so ordering, the grain men were shocked somewhat rudely out of their complacency.

Following up this preliminary victory, the Manitoba Grain Growers turned to the Manitoba Government and demanded that the charter under which the Grain Exchange operated be amended in certain particulars. The deputation from the Grain Growers met the Committee on Agriculture, the House being in session, and asked that the powers of the charter be limited so that business would be conducted on an equitable basis between buyer and producer. They asked that the Exchange be allowed to set no limit as to the number of persons who might enjoy its privileges, the question of the reputability of such persons to be decided by a majority of the members and that a seat purchased for the use of any firm or corporation should entitle that firm to the privileges of the Exchange even though registration of membership was under the name of an individual; also that the right to membership should include the right to delegate the trading powers to anyone in the employ of the firm or corporation.

The Grain Growers also asked that arbitrary interference with the business methods employed by individual firms or corporations and inquisitional inquiry into such be prohibited; also that the penalties and disabilities against those breaking the common rules and the maximum-price rule be abolished; that the right to define the eligibility of a person as an employee or fix a limit to salary in any way be denied; also that the expulsion of no member should be considered final until assented to by the Minister of Agriculture and that all by-laws should receive the assent of the Lieutenant-Governor in Council before becoming legal and binding.

The farmers asked that the Government have full access to the minute books, papers and accounts of the Grain Exchange and that provision be made for the public to have free access to a gallery overlooking the trading room during the sessions of the Exchange so that the transactions occurring might be observed and the prices disseminated through the public press. They further wished to see gambling in futures made a criminal offence.

Roderick McKenzie, Secretary of the Manitoba Association, told how the existing Grain Exchange had about three hundred members, of whom one hundred were active and fifty-seven of these active members represented the elevator interests. He said that the interests of the fifty-seven were looked after by twelve elevator men in the Exchange and that these twelve men agreed so well that they allowed one of their number to send out the price which should be paid for wheat for the day.

The Committee on Agriculture promised to consider the requests and later, when they met to do so, members of the Grain Exchange attended in force to present their side of the case. They claimed that a great deal of the trouble existing between the producer and the Grain Exchange was due to misconception of the Exchange's methods of action. The Exchange was only a factor in the grain business and under their charter they were allowed to make by-laws and regulations, these being necessary in such an intricate business as handling grain.

The wiring of prices to country points was done by the North-West Grain Dealers' Association, which had nothing to do with the Exchange but was a distinct and separate organization for the purpose of running elevators at country points as cheaply as possible. The highest possible prices were quoted and the plan was merely to avoid duplicate wiring.

The grain men claimed that it was impossible to handle the wheat of the country unless futures were allowed while to carry on its business properly the Exchange must have the power to say who should be members and otherwise to regulate its business. If the producer was getting full value for his wheat why should the Grain Exchange be interfered with?

The Exchange was willing that its membership should be extended. Their books always would be open to Government inspection in future and they would also repeal the rule regarding track-buyers' salaries. The press was already admitted and it would be found that when the new building which the Exchange was erecting was completed there would be a gallery for the use of the public during trading hours.

If the Legislature were to amend the charter, declared the Exchange's spokesman, the Exchange would demand that the charter be cancelled *in toto* and a receiver appointed to distribute the assets. The Exchange was tired of being branded thieves and robbers and they should be let alone to do their business. If this were not satisfactory, then they wished to be put out of business altogether.

The Grain Growers protested that it was not their desire to have the charter cancelled. They were not blind to the usefulness of the Exchange if it were properly managed and all they asked was that this organization be compelled to do what was right. The reason the Exchange had admitted the Grain Growers' Grain Company, the farmers claimed, was so that they could have it under discipline, being afraid of a combination of farmers in the interests of the producer. The farmers had lost confidence in the manipulations of the Exchange and wanted official protection.

The question of declaring deals in futures to be a criminal offence was outside provincial jurisdiction and the farmers withdrew that part of the request. They wished everything else to stand, however.

At this juncture a recommendation was made that a conference be held between the Government, the Grain Growers, the Exchange, reeves of municipalities, bankers, railroads, etc., for discussion of everything pertaining to the handling of wheat, including amendments to the Grain Exchange charter. The idea appealed to the Premier and before the Committee he pledged that the resolutions passed at the proposed conference would be converted into legislation.

After adopting the Agricultural Committee's report the Government did not act independently regarding the suggested charter amendments, as the farmers had hoped they would; instead, the whole thing was shelved, pending the suggested conference. When this conference was held in the latter part of February, however, the Government was duly impressed by the earnestness of the Grain Growers. Many strong speeches were made, including one powerful arraignment by J. W. Scallion, of Virden, whose energetic leadership had earned him the title: "Father of all the Grain Growers." The Government promised to amend the Exchange charter at the next session of the Legislature.

The activity of the Manitoba Grain Growers' Association was putting a new face upon the struggle of the Grain Growers' Grain Company for the restoration of their trading privileges on the floor of the Exchange. It demonstrated that the farmers could act in concert if occasion arose and that the Grain Growers' Associations were in accord with the principles for which the farmers' trading company was fighting. When, therefore, the Manitoba Association took a hand in the matter by officially urging the Manitoba Government to assist in restoring the Company to its former position on the Exchange in order that it could enjoy the rights of the seat for which it had paid, the Government was forced to take action.

It is doubtful if a Minister of the Crown in Manitoba ever had been called upon to make a more remarkable official statement than that which now appeared in print in connection with this matter. In the absence of Hon. R. P. Roblin it became the duty of the Acting-Premier to make it. Hon. Robert Rogers, then Minister of Public Works in the Manitoba Government, was the official head of the Government in the Premier's absence and in the *Winnipeg Telegram* of April 4th, 1907, the statement appeared as follows:

"The action of the Council of the Winnipeg Grain Exchange in refusing trading privileges to the Grain Growers' Grain

Company is regarded by the Government as an arbitrary exercise of the powers conferred upon them (the Exchange) through their charter from the Legislative Assembly of Manitoba, and unless remedied by the Exchange, the Government will call the Legislature together during the present month for the purpose of remedying the conditions by Legislative amendments."

On April 15th the farmers' trading company was admitted once more to the full privileges of their seat on the Exchange.

The case against the three members of the Grain Exchange, who had been indicted under Section 498 of the Criminal Code, came to trial in the Assize Court a week later, on April 22nd, before Judge Phippen. It was now a matter for Crown prosecution and under direction of the Attorney-General, R. A. Bonnar, K.C., proceeded vigorously. The Grain Growers claimed that the Exchange had rules and regulations which had been carried out in restraint of trade and that in combination with the North-West Grain Dealers' Association there had been a practice of restricting the price to be paid for grain to certain daily figures, sent out by the parties conspiring.

Also, they expected to show that there had been a combine in existence between the elevator companies so that there was no competition in the buying of grain at certain points while there was an agreement that only a certain amount of street wheat would be received at the various elevators, the whole thing amounting to the restriction of wheat buying within certain limits fixed by the combination of the buyers who belonged to the combine—this to the consequent barring out of the small buyer from the trade. The latter, the Grain Growers argued, was prevented from buying by the rule which called for the payment of a salary to track buyers and prohibited the hiring of men on commission; there were points where the quantity of grain offered for sale was too limited to justify the payment of a fifty-dollar salary to the buyer.

Another point of complaint was that the Grain Exchange membership was restricted to three hundred, the members having agreed among themselves that no more seats be added although all present seats were sold and many more might be sold to eligible citizens.

Also, claimed the prosecution, there was a practical boycott of expelled members in that the members of the Exchange were forbidden to deal with expelled members; it was practically impossible to do business in grain in Western Canada unless connected with the Grain Exchange, one firm having experienced this difficulty.

The rule which barred the purchasing of grain on track during the hours of trading on the Exchange was, they would endeavor to show, an act in restraint of trade and the three men under indictment, the prosecution hoped to prove, had been active in the enactment of the alleged illegal by-laws of the Grain Exchange.

Prior to the enactment of these obnoxious laws of the Exchange the farmers had been sought by the buyers, whereas since the rules had been established the farmer must seek the purchaser. While the prices given out were fixed by the Grain Exchange in what was claimed to be open competition, the prosecution intended to show that it was a gambling transaction pure and simple, the price-fixing being nothing more than the guess of the men who acted for their own gain.

The trial lasted for a month, during which time a great many witnesses were examined—grain men and farmers—and the whole grain trade reviewed. The array of legal talent for the defence was very imposing and the case attracted much attention because, aside from its interest to the grain trade and the farming population, it promised to test the particular and somewhat obscure section of the Criminal Code under which the indictment was laid. At one stage of the proceedings the tension in court became so high and witnesses so unwilling that upon reproval by the court regarding his examination, leading counsel for the Grain Growers picked up his bag and walked out in protest, willing to risk punishment for the breach of etiquette rather than remain. After the Grain Growers' executive and counsel had conferred with the Government, however, the Grain Growers' counsel was prevailed upon to resume the case.

The finding of the court did not come as much of a surprise; for it was apparent before the trial ended that the section of the Code was considered ambiguous by the presiding Judge. The latter held that all restraints suggested by the evidence were agreed to, whether justifiably or not, as business regulations and before finding the defendants guilty these restraints must appear to be "undue," according to his reading of the section. It was necessary to respect the right of a particular trade or business or of a particular class of traders to protect their property by regulations and agreements so long as the public interests were not thereby "unduly" impaired; to the Judge's mind there was no question that the public had not been *unduly* affected.

After reviewing the case the Judge held that the gravamen of the whole charge hung upon the Commission Rule of the Exchange—that one cent commission per bushel should be made in handling grain; so that the price paid would be the price at the terminal (Fort William) less the freight and one cent per bushel commission, neither more nor less.

Witnesses agreed that this was the lowest profit on which the business could live. Fort William prices were the highest the world's markets could justify. Owing to the presence in the statute of the word, "unduly," therefore, the Judge could not find the defendants guilty.

The Grain Growers were much dissatisfied with the decision; for they believed that they had adduced evidence to support their case and did not relish losing it on a technicality. Appeal was made, therefore; but the appeal court upheld the judgment of the assize court.

Apparently, deduced the farmers, this meant that men could conspire to create monopolies by driving all competitors out of business so long as they did not do it out of pure malice— so long as they justified it on the grounds of "personal interest"—so long as the things they did were not "malicious restraints, unconnected with any business relations of the accused!" In other words, if men merely conspired to advance their own business interests they committed no offence under the then existing law; to be liable to punishment they must be actuated by malice.

So that all the turmoil and talk, court proceedings and conferences, deputations and denunciations, evidence and evasions—all the excitement of the past few months practically left conditions just where they were. For the amendments to the Grain Exchange charter would not materialize till the Legislature met again next year.

But there was one spot where the clouds had rifted and the light shone through. The Grain Growers' Grain Company had won back its place on the Exchange. More and more the farmers began to pin their faith to their little fighting trading company "at the front." It appeared to be the concentration point for the fire of enemy guns. In all probability hostilities would break out anew, but the men in charge were good men—loyal and determined; they could be relied upon to take a full-sized whack at every difficulty which raised its head.

The first of these to threaten was on the way.

[1] Now Chief Justice Haultain.

CHAPTER X

PRINTERS' INK

The fewer the voices on the side of truth, the more distinct and strong must be your own.

—Channing.

As the farmers saw it, there was no reason in the world why the bank should do what it did. The Company had closed its first year with net profits sufficient to declare a seven per cent. cash dividend and the profits would have been augmented greatly had it not been for the heavy interest payments which accrued on the unusual overdrafts imposed by special conditions. In spite of their extremely limited resources and the handicaps forced upon them, the volume of business transacted had exceeded $1,700,000 during the first ten months that the farmers had been in business; their paid-up capital had been approximately eleven thousand dollars of which over seven thousand had been required for organization outlay. The number of shareholders had nearly doubled during the ten months and everything was pointing to rapid advancement. The Company had been a good customer of the bank, which had received about $10,000 in interest. The security offered for their line of credit was unquestioned.

Yet the new directors had scarcely settled into place for the approaching busy season before, without warning, the bank notified them that they wished to close out the account.

When men set themselves up in business they expect to have to compete for their share of trade. The farmers did not expect to find their path lined with other grain dealers cheering them forward and waving their hats. They expected competition of the keenest. What they could not anticipate, however, was the lengths to which the fight might go or the methods that might be adopted to put their Agency out of business altogether.

Hitherto the grain grower had been in the background when it came to marketing and handling grain. He was away out in the country somewhere—busy plowing, busy seeding, busy harvesting, busy something-or-other. He was a Farm Hand who so "tuckered himself out" during daylight that he was glad to pry off his wrinkled boots and lie down when it got dark in order to yank them on again, when the rooster crowed at dawn, for the purpose of "tuckering himself out" all over again. It was true that without him there would have been no grain to handle; equally true that without the grain dealers the farmer would have been in difficulty if he tried to hunt up individual consumers to buy his wheat. The farmer interfering in the established grain trade was something new and it was not to be supposed that when the surprise of it wore off things were not liable to happen.

The farmer was quick to infer that the action of the bank in cutting off the trading company's credit without apparent cause was another move of the opposing forces. It was so palpably a vital spot at which to strike.

This time, however, the threatening cloud evaporated almost as soon as it appeared. The manager, W. H. Machaffie, resigned and assumed the management of another bank. He was a far-sighted financier, Mr. Machaffie, and almost the first account he sought for the Home Bank was that of the Grain Growers' Grain Company. The Home Bank was new in the West and in the East it had been an old loan company without big capitalistic interests, its funds being derived mostly from small depositors; but while at that time it was not among the wealthiest banking institutions of the country, it was quite able to supply full credit facilities.

The opportunity for the farmers' company and the young bank to get together to mutual advantage was too good to be overlooked. Under the banking laws of Canada valuable special privileges are granted in view of the important part which the banks play in the country's development. Government returns indicate that the greater part of the business done by banks is carried on upon their deposits. If the working people and the farmers, as is generally accepted, form the majority of these depositors of money in banks, then were not many loans which went to monopolistic interests being used against the very people who furnished the money? If the farmers could acquire stock in a bank of their own, would they not be in a position to finance their own requirements rather than those of corporations which might be obtaining unreasonable profits from the people at large? Such an investment would be safe and productive at the same time that it strengthened the farmers' hands in their effort to do their own trading.

With all this in view the directors of the Grain Growers' Grain Company made a heavy investment in Home Bank stock and were appointed sole brokers to sell a large block of the bank's stock to Western farmers, working men and merchants. On the sale of this they were to receive a commission which would, they expected, be enough to cover the expense of placing the stock. As the business expanded the Company would be assured of an extended line of credit as it was needed.

And the business certainly was expanding. Although the prospects for the new crop were not as bright as they had been the year before, a substantial increase in the amount of grain they would handle—owing to the increase in the number of shareholders—was anticipated by the management. They were not prepared, however, for the heavy volume that poured in upon them when the crop began to move; it was double that of their first season and the office staff was hard pressed to keep pace with the rising work. There now seemed no reason to believe that the success of the farmers' venture was any longer in doubt so far as the commercial side of it was concerned.

But the President and directors had in mind a much broader objective. It was not enough that the farmer should receive a few more cents per bushel for his grain.

"We must bear clearly in mind," warned T. A. Crerar, "that there are still those interests who would delight in nothing more than in our failure and destruction. A great many improvements require yet to be made in our system of handling grain. The struggle for the bringing about of those reforms is not by any means accomplished. As a great class of farmers, composing the most important factor in the progress and development of our country, we must learn the lesson that we must organize and work together to secure those legislative and economic reforms necessary to well-being. In the day of our prosperity we must not forget that there are yet many wrongs to be righted and that true happiness and success in life cannot be measured by the wealth we acquire. In the mad, debasing struggle for material riches and pleasure, which is so characteristic of our age, we often neglect and let go to decay the finer and higher side of

Hopkins Moorhouse

our nature and lose thereby that power of sympathy with our fellows which finds expression in lending them a helping hand and in helping in every good work which tends to increase human happiness and lessen human misery. In keeping this in view we keep in mind that high ideal which will make our organization not alone a material success but also a factor in changing those conditions which now tend to stifle the best that is in humanity."

An important step towards the upholding of these ideals was now taken by the directors. The President and the Vice-President happened to be in a little printshop one day, looking over the proof of a pamphlet which the Company was about to issue, when the former picked up a little school journal which was just off the press for the Teachers' Association.

"Why can't we get out a little journal like that?" he wondered. "It would be a great help to our whole movement."

About this time the Company was approached by a Winnipeg farm paper which devoted a page to the doings of the grain growers.

"If you'll help us to get subscriptions amongst the farmers," said the publisher, "we'll devote more space still to the doings of the grain growers."

"But why should we build up another man's paper for him?" argued the President. "Why can't we get out a journal for ourselves?"

The idea grew more insistent the longer it was entertained, and although at first E. A. Partridge, who was on the directorate, was opposed to such a venture, he finally agreed that it would be of untold assistance to the farmers if they had a paper of their own to voice their ideals. The logical editor for the new undertaking was E. A. Partridge, of course, and accordingly he began to gather material for the first issue of a paper, to be called the *Grain Growers' Guide*.

Partridge had a few ideas of his own that had lived with him for a long time. On occasion he had introduced some of them to his friends with characteristic eloquence and the eloquence of E. A. Partridge on a favorite theme was something worth listening to; also, he gave his auditors much to think about and sometimes got completely beyond their depth. It was then that some of them were forced to shake their heads at theories which appeared to them to be so idealistic that their practical consummation belonged to a future generation.

In connection with this new paper it was Partridge's idea to issue it as a weekly and as the official organ of the grain growers' trading company instead of the grain growers' movement as a whole. He thought, too, that it would be advisable to join hands with *The Voice*, which was the organ of the Labor unions. The President and the other officers could not agree that any of these was wise at the start; it would be better, they thought, to creep before trying to walk, to issue the paper as a monthly at first and to have it the official organ of the Grain Growers' Associations rather than the trading company alone.

This failure of his associates to see the wisdom of his plan to amalgamate with the organ of the Labor unions was a great disappointment to Partridge; for he had been working towards this consummation for some time, devoutly wished it and considered the time opportune for such a move. He believed it to be of vital importance to "the Cause" and its future. In October he had met with an unfortunate accident, having fallen from his binder and so injured his foot in the machinery that amputation was necessary; he was in no condition to undertake new and arduous duties in organizing a publishing proposition as he was still suffering greatly from his injury. On the verge of a nervous breakdown, it required only the upsetting of the plans he had cherished to make him give up altogether and he resigned the editorship of the new magazine after getting out the first number.

"I'm too irritable to get along with anybody in an office," he declared. "I know I'm impatient and all that, boys. You'd better send for McKenzie to come in from Brandon and edit the paper."

This suggestion of his editorial successor seemed to the others to be a good one; for Roderick McKenzie had been Secretary of the Manitoba Grain Growers' Association from the first and had been a prime mover in its activities as well as wielding considerable influence in the other two prairie provinces where he was well known and appreciated. He was well posted, McKenzie.

So the Vice-President wired him to come down to Winnipeg at once.

Yes, he was well posted in the farming business, Rod. McKenzie. He had learned it in the timber country before he took to it in the land of long grass. At eleven years of age he was plowing with a yoke of oxen on the stump lands of Huron, helping his father to scratch a living out of the bush farm for a family of nine and between whiles attending a little log schoolhouse, going on cedar-gum expeditions, getting lost in the bush and indulging in other pioneer pastimes.

Along in 1877, when people were talking a lot about Dakota as a farming country, McKenzie took a notion to go West; but he preferred to stay under the British flag and Winnipeg was his objective. A friend of his was running a flour-mill at Gladstone (then called Palestine), Manitoba, and young McKenzie decided to take a little walk out that way to visit him. It was a wade, rather than a walk! It was the year the country was flooded and during the first thirty days after his arrival he could count only three consecutive days without rain. In places the water was up to his hips and when he reached the flour-mill there was four feet of water inside of it.

Such conditions were abnormal, of course, and due to lack of settlement and drainage. After helping to build the first railway through the country Roderick McKenzie eventually located his farm near Brandon and so far as the rich land and the climate were concerned he was entirely satisfied.

Not so with the early marketing of his grain, though. He disposed of two loads of wheat at one of the elevators in Brandon one day and was given a grade and price which he considered fair enough. When he came in with two more loads of the same kind of wheat next day, however, the elevator man told him that he had sent a sample to Winnipeg and found out that it was not grading the grade he had given him the day before.

"The train service wouldn't allow of such fast work, sir," said Roderick McKenzie. "I suppose you sent it by wire!" He picked up the reins. "That five cents a bushel you want me to give you looks just as good in my pocket as in yours."

So he drove up town where the other buyers were and three of them looked at the wheat but refused to give a price for it. One of them was a son of the first elevator man to whom he had gone and, said he:

"The Old Man gave you a knockdown for it, didn't he?"

"Yes, but—"

"Well, we're not going to bid against him and if you want to sell it at all, haul it back to him."

As there was nothing else he could do under the conditions that prevailed, McKenzie was forced to pocket his loss without recourse.

With such experiences it is scarcely necessary to say that when the grain growers' movement started in Manitoba Roderick McKenzie occupied a front seat. He was singled out at once for a place on the platform and was elected Secretary of the Brandon branch of the Association. At the annual convention of the Manitoba locals he was made Secretary of the Provincial Association, a position which he filled until 1916, when he became Secretary of the Canadian Council of Agriculture.

His activities in the interests of the Association have made him a well-known figure in many circles. From the first he had been very much in favor of the farmers' trading company and only the restrictions of his official position with the Association had prevented him from taking a more prominent part in its affairs. As it was, the benefit of his experience was frequently sought.

McKenzie was plowing in the field when the boy from the telegraph office reached him with John Kennedy's message.

"They don't say what they want me for; but I guess I'm wanted or they wouldn't send a telegram—Haw! Back you!" And like Cincinnatus at the call of the State in the "brave days of old," McKenzie unhitched the horses and leaving the plow where it stood, made for the house, packed his grip and caught the next train for Winnipeg.

John Kennedy met him at the station.

"What's wrong?" demanded the Secretary of the Manitoba Grain Growers' Association at once. "I came right along as soon as I got your wire, Kennedy. What's up now?"

"The editor of the *Grain Growers' Guide*. Partridge wants you to take his place."

"ME? Why, I never edited anything in my life!" cried McKenzie, standing stock still on the platform.

"Pshaw! Come along," laughed Kennedy reassuringly. "You'll be alright. It ain't hard to do."

CHAPTER XI

FROM THE RED RIVER VALLEY
TO THE FOOTHILLS

It ain't the guns or armament nor the funds that they can
pay,
But the close co-operation that makes them win the day;
It ain't the individual, nor the army as a whole,
But the everlastin' team-work of every bloomin' soul!

—Kipling.

At one of the early grain growers' conventions it had been
voiced as an ideal that there were three things which the
farmers' movement needed—first, a trading company to sell
their products (with ultimately, it might be, the cheaper
distribution of farm supplies); second, a bank in which they
could own stock; third, a paper that would publish the
farmers' views. So that if the new Executive of the Company
had done little else than break ground for better financial
arrangements and a farmers' own paper, their record for the
year would have shown progress.

But when the second annual meeting of the Company was
held they were able to show that the volume of farmers' grain
handled was almost five million bushels, double that of the

first year, while the net profits amounted to over thirty thousand dollars. The number of farmer shareholders had increased to nearly three thousand with applications on file for another twelve hundred and a steady awakening of interest among the farmers was to be noticed all over the West. All this in spite of the general shortage of money, a reduced total crop yield and the keenest competition from rival grain interests.

It had been apparent to the directors that if the business grew as conditions seemed to warrant it doing, it would require to be highly organized. Bit by bit the service to the farmer was being widened. For instance, the nucleus of a Claims Department had been established during the year; for under the laws governing the Canadian railway companies the latter were required to deliver to terminal elevators the amount of grain a farmer loaded into a car and to leave the car in a suitable condition to receive grain. The official weights at the terminal were unquestioned and if a farmer could furnish reasonable evidence of the quantity of grain he had loaded, any leakage in transit would furnish a claim case against the railway. During six months the farmers' company had collected for its shippers nearly two thousand dollars in such claims, a beginning sufficient to illustrate that the Company was destined to serve the farmers in many practical ways if they would only stand behind it.

IF the farmers would stand behind it! But would they? It was a question which was forever popping up to obscure the future. Many tongues were busy with inuendo to belittle what the farmers had accomplished already and to befog their efforts to advance still farther. At every shipping point in the West industrious little mallets were knocking away on the Xylophone of Doubt, all playing the same tune: "Just Kiss Yourself Good-Bye!" No farmers' business organization ever had been a success in the past and none ever could be.

This new trading venture was going to go off with a loud bang one of these fine days and every farmer who had shipped grain to it would stand a first-class chance of losing it. You betcha! The Grain Growers' Associations mightn't be so bad; yes, they'd done some good. But this concern in the grain business—run by a few men, wasn't it? Well, say, does a cat go by a saucer of cream without taking a lick? "Farmers' company" they called it, eh? Go and tell it to your grandmother!

The worst of it was that in many localities were farmers who believed this very suggestion already—that the Company belonged to the men at the head of its affairs. Discouraged by past failures and without much respect for the dignity of their occupation, their attitude towards the Company was almost automatic. That it was a great co-operative movement of their class, designed to improve economic and social conditions, was something quite out of their grasp. And upon these strings, already out of tune, elevator men strummed diligently in an effort to create discord.

From the first it had been like that. Friends who would speak a good word for the struggling venture at the time it was most needed were about as scarce as horns on a horse. On the other hand the organizers ran across "the knockers" at every turn. A traveller for one of the milling companies, for instance, happened to get into conversation on the train with E. A. Partridge one day. The latter was a stranger to him and he naturally supposed he was talking to "just a farmer." The subject of conversation was the grain trade and this traveller began to make a few remarks about the "little grain company" that had started up.

"What about that company?" asked Partridge with visible interest. "I've heard a lot about it."

"Oh, it's just a little dinky affair," laughed the traveller. "They've got a little office about ten feet square and they actually have a typewriter! They get a car or two a month. Don't amount to anything."

For a full hour he kept the chutes open and filled his interested auditor with all the latest brands of misrepresentation and ridicule. He explained why it was that the farmers' effort was nothing but a joke and how foolish it would be for any farmer to send business to it. He was a good salesman, this traveller, and he was sure he had "sold" this rather intelligent hayseed when he got to the end of his talk and his station was called.

"I've really enjoyed this," assured Partridge gratefully. "As a farmer I'm naturally interested in that sort of thing, you know, and I've got a particular interest in that little grain company. My name is Partridge and I only want to say—"

But the traveller had grabbed his club bag and was off down the aisle as fast as he could go. Salesmanship is punctuated by "psychological moments" and good salesmen always know when to leave. He did not look around. His ears were very red.

It was funny. No, it wasn't, either! Lies about the Company, thought the then President, would travel a thousand miles before the Truth could get its boots on! It was not a matter for amusement at all.

As the "little dinky affair" became a competitor of increasing strength in the grain trade the efforts of a section of the grain men, particularly the elevator interests, to discredit it among the farmers became more and more marked. While the farmers' company was not openly attacked, influences nevertheless were constantly at work to undermine in roundabout

Hopkins Moorhouse

ways. The elevator men were in a strong position to fight hard and they pressed every advantage. At practically every shipping point they had agents whose business it was to secure shipments of grain in car lots as well as buying on street. Many of these men were very popular locally and as individuals were good fellows, well liked by their farmer friends. A rebate on the charges for loading grain through an elevator or the mere fact that letting the elevator have it saved the bother of writing a letter—these were excellent inducements to the unthinking farmer, and when added to this was the element of personal acquaintance with the buyer, it was hard to refuse.

For your farmer is a man of simple code. He is not versed in subterfuge and diplomacy. He takes words at their face value, unless he distrusts you, just as he hands them out himself. He lives a clean, honest life and earns his money. If in some cases his viewpoint is narrowed by treading much in the same furrows, it is at least an honest viewpoint in which he really believes. And one of the things in which the average farmer prides himself is that he will "never go back on a friend." Even a red Indian would not do that!

In selling to the elevator these same farmers probably had no intention of unfriendliness to the farmers' trading company. They hoped to see it succeed but did not appreciate their individual responsibility in the matter or realize that while their own personal defection represented a loss to the Company of just one shipment, the loss became vital when multiplied many times all along the line. And the Company had no agent on the ground to argue this out, face to face.

Although many requests for the appointment of such local agents reached the office, the directors decided that it would be poor policy as it would mean appointing agents every-where and abuses might develop. It would be easy under such a system for an impression to get abroad that favoritism was being shown in appointments; jealousies and disappointments might be the result. On the other hand, one of the greatest sources of strength which the Company could foster would be a sense of individual responsibility among its farmer shareholders—each shareholder an agent for his own grain and that of his non-member neighbors, each doing his part to keep down the handling cost of his grain and build up his own company. In the meantime it were better to lose some grain than run the risk of disrupting the whole movement—to let the elevators enjoy their advantage until it became a nullity by education of the farmer himself.

Such educational work was already a regular part of the routine. Pamphlets and circulars were issued from time to time, dealing with prevailing conditions, advocating amendments to the Grain Act, etc., and explaining the need for government ownership of elevators. The feeling that the Provincial governments should acquire and operate all storage facilities in the way of elevators and warehouses was spreading rapidly among farmers and business men.

In the second year the Grain Growers' Grain Company began to export several small shipments, more for the sake of the experience than anything else. A very extensive line of credit was necessary to go into the export business and, until the arrangement with the Home Bank developed this, their hands were tied in the matter of exporting for themselves. Their third year in business, though, found their financial relations so improved that they were able to do a considerable and profitable business in the exporting of grain, thereby advancing definitely towards one objective which the farmers had had from the first. Most of the grain which the Company handled in this way was sold to exporters in the Eastern States and in Eastern Canada, this method being found more satisfactory than selling direct to buyers in the

Old Country at this time.

In spite of everything, therefore, things were swinging the farmers' way. The whole Farmers' Movement was expanding, solidifying, particularly in Alberta, which for so long had been primarily a cattle country. Grain production was now increasing rapidly in this Province of the Foothills and Chinooks and the future shipment of Alberta grain to the Pacific Coast and thence via the new Panama Canal route was a live topic. Owing to special conditions prevailing in the farthest west of the three Prairie Provinces the Grain Growers' movement there did not solidify until 1909 into its final cohesion under the name, "United Farmers of Alberta."

Prior to this the farmers of Alberta had been organized into two groups—the Canadian Society of Equity and the Alberta Farmers' Association. The first had its beginnings among some farmers from the United States—mostly from Nebraska and Dakota—who settled near Edmonton and who in their former home had been members of the American Society of Equity. These farmers in 1904-5 organized some branches of the American Society after arrival in the new land and, becoming ambitious, formed the Canadian Society of Equity with the idea of owning and controlling their own flour and lumber mills and what not. For this Purpose they got together a concern called "The Canadian Society of Equity, Limited," and bought a timber limit, so called. They secured shareholders in all parts of Alberta and the concern went to smash in 1907, this unfortunate failure making doubly shy those farmers who had been bitten.

Meanwhile, in 1905, the members of the local branch of the American Society of equity which had been established at Clover Bar had reached the conclusion that the work of the Society did not meet the requirements of conditions in Alberta and that it was not desirable to have the farmers of the province organized into two camps—the Society of Equity on one hand and the Alberta branches of the Territorial Grain Growers' Association on the other. Especially now that the Territories were to be established into the Provinces of Saskatchewan and Alberta, it was desirable that reorganization and a change of name take place. Accordingly the Clover Bar branch of the American Society of Equity and the Strathcona branch of the Territorial Grain Growers' Association got their heads together on a proposal to amalgamate into one farmers' organization under the name, Alberta Farmers' Association.

Under the impression that this was a veiled scheme of the Grain Growers to swallow their organization whole, the Society of Equity turned down the idea of amalgamation. The Clover Bar farmers withdrew from the Society and joined the Strathcona Grain Growers in forming the nucleus of a provincial farmers' association as planned.

Owing to the mixed nature of Alberta's agricultural population and to the general distrust of farmers' organizations the new Alberta Farmers' Association faced a difficult situation. But the principles laid down by their leaders were so fair, so sane and broad-minded, that in two years the Association became an influence in almost every line of trade in the province. They organized a very successful seed fair, a feature of which was a meeting to discuss improvement of the market for live stock, especially hogs; this resulted in the appointment of a Pork Commission. At their convention in 1906 the Association took stand on such important matters as the special grading of Alberta Hard Winter Wheat, the establishment of a terminal elevator at the Pacific Coast, of a pork-packing and beef-chilling plant by the Provincial Government, etc. In the discussion of everything affecting the welfare of the farmers the Association played an important part and it was at their request that the Provincial Government sent an agent to investigate the markets of British Columbia with the idea of closer relations.

A second attempt to amalgamate with the Canadian Society of Equity, which had succeeded the American Society, had fallen through and there were still two farmers' organizations in the Province of Alberta. However, with the progress being made with the Provincial Government in connection with the pork-packing and beef-chilling plant and with the Dominion Government in regard to government ownership of terminal elevators, the farmers as a whole began to see the need of closer union. Such wide measures as a system of government-owned internal elevators were bringing the farmers of all three Western provinces into closer conference and in 1908 the feeling in favor of amalgamation of all Alberta farmers into one organization began to crystallize.

Finally in September a conference was held between representatives of the Alberta Farmers' Association and the Canadian Society of Equity. The constitution drafted at this conference was submitted to the annual conventions of both bodies at Edmonton on January 13th, 1909. The following morning the delegates of the Canadian Society of Equity marched from their hall to the convention of the Alberta Farmers' Association and amid great cheers the two became one under the name, United Farmers of Alberta, with "Equity" as their motto, and with a strong coalition directorate.[1]

Until now each of the organizations had had its separate official organ; but on amalgamation these were dropped and the *Grain Growers' Guide* adopted as the official organ for Alberta. First published under the auspices of the Manitoba Grain Growers' Association, the *Guide* now represented the farmers' movement in all three provinces. The wisdom of its establishment was being proved steadily. Its circulation was gathering momentum with every issue. It was now coming out as a weekly and its pages were filled with valuable information for the farmer on every subject dealing with the marketing of his produce. Also it was proving a wonderful educator on such large questions as government ownership of elevators, the tariff, control of public service corporations and so forth. The farmer was getting information which he had never been able to obtain before and he was getting it without distortion, uncolored by convenient imagination, plain as Fact itself.

An up-to-date printing plant had been installed to print the *Guide* and do a general job-printing business, and this was organized as a separate company under the name of the "Public Press, Limited."

In addition to all the difficulties which usually attend the building of a publishing enterprise to success, the farmers' own journal had to face many more which were due to the special nature of its policies. Manufacturers who disapproved of its attitude on the tariff, for instance, refused for a long while to use its advertising columns. Each year as the *Guide's* struggle went on there was an annual deficit and had it not been for the grants with which the Grain Growers' Grain Company came to its rescue, the paper must have gone under. For this financial assistance the farmers' trading company got no return except the satisfaction of knowing that the money could not be spent to better advantage in the interests of Western farmers.

With the rapid developments in Alberta and the probable future shipment of Alberta grain via the Panama Canal route, branch offices were being opened at Calgary by Winnipeg grain dealers. Not to be behind in the matter of service, the farmers' company followed suit. A Seed Branch Department to supply good seed grain was another improvement in service and the farmers by this time were taking a keen interest in their trading organization.

When the third annual meeting came around, there was no longer any doubt that a farmers' business organization *could* succeed—that this venture of the Grain Growers was *not* going to go off with a loud bang—at least, not yet.

But, as the President remarked, it seemed that they had no more than touched the fringe of what remained to be accomplished. One of the immediate questions pressing for solution, he considered, was government ownership of elevators.

"Our Company's experience has demonstrated completely," he said, "that our grain marketing conditions can never reach a proper basis as long as the elevators necessary for that marketing are allowed to remain in private hands for private gain. The Grain Growers' Associations are the one thing above everything else that stands between the farmer and the power of merciless corporations. They have undoubtedly been the greatest shield this Company has had since its organization; they have helped the Company to prove, far beyond any question of doubt, the advantages of co-operation."

And what had the elevator men to say about all this? Surely these farmers were becoming a menace! At the present rate of speed another three years would see them in control of the grain business and was that good for the grain business? Was it good for the farmer? The elevator men did not think so.

Strangely enough, they were not worrying greatly about government ownership. They were more interested in the fact that the volume of grain which had flowed so faithfully all these years was being split up by all these commission men—these hangers-on who invested little or no capital but necked right up to the profits of the trade as if they owned the whole business!

Trouble was brewing on the Winnipeg Grain Exchange—had been for some time.

Then one day word reached the office of the Grain Growers' Grain Company that by a majority vote the Grain Exchange had suspended, for a period of one year, the Commission Rule under which grain was handled.

Thus did things come to a showdown.

[1] See Appendix—Par. 10.

CHAPTER XII

THE SHOWDOWN

It's scarcely in a body's power
Tae keep at times frae being sour
Tae see how things are shared.

—Robert Burns.

A fight was on between the elevator interests and the commission merchants of the Winnipeg Grain Exchange—a fight for existence. For, with the Commission Rule of the Exchange eliminated, those firms which handled grain on a straight commission basis would be forced to meet the competition of the elevator buyers and the chances were they would be forced to handle grain at a loss; the best they could hope for would be to cover their costs.

It will be remembered that this Commission Rule, established in 1899, was that a charge of one cent commission per bushel should be made for handling grain and that all members of the Exchange dealing in grain must show that the price paid was the price at the terminal (Fort William) less the freight and one cent per bushel commission. This commission could be neither more nor less than one cent; for at that time it was felt that business could not be done, offices maintained and an efficient and reliable service given for less. It was a charge which both farmers and grain men considered fair and reasonable.

The trouble in the Exchange started when the commission men claimed the right to have country agents and to pay them on a commission basis of one-quarter cent per bushel. The elevator companies were able to buy at elevator points through their salaried representatives but the commission men were prohibited from having country agents except on a salary basis, and this they could not afford, handling grain on commission.

For some years past there had been considerable dissatisfaction among Exchange members in regard to the operation of the Commission rule, doubt being entertained that all the members were keeping good faith in the collection of the full commission charge of one cent to non-members of the Exchange and one-half cent per bushel to members on country consigned and purchased grain. Although the Council of the Exchange had held many special meetings in an endeavor to find a remedy and to investigate the charges, the results had not been very marked owing to the difficulty of securing the evidence to support such charges.

This was given as a reason for the doing away with the one cent commission restriction altogether for a trial period of one year. Thereby the trade was put on a "free for all" basis, as the President of the Exchange then in office pointed out. It meant that Exchange members were "enabled to pay owners of grain in the country any price they desired without regard to actual market values as regularly established on the floor of the Exchange." It was the personal opinion of the President that to preserve stable markets with uniformity and discipline amongst Exchange members a commission rule was absolutely necessary and he predicted that perhaps in a short while, after the suspension of the Commission Rule had been given a fair trial, the Exchange might see its way clear to rescind the suspension.

"Just so," nodded the commission men among themselves. "The logical and certain result will be the weeding out of the commission men and track buyers, who give practically the only element of competition that exists in the trade! One of the curses of our Canadian commercialism is the strong tendency to monopoly and this looks like an effort to create an absolute elevator monopoly of the grain trade, which is the staple industry of the country."

But if the small dealers on the Exchange were aroused, what about the farmers' trading company? They did business on a commission basis only and with the elevators offering to handle the farmers' grain for nothing, or next door to it, what would happen? Would the farmer be "unable to see past his nose," as was predicted? Would he forget the conditions of the early days and grab for a present saving of five or ten dollars per car? If the farmers did not stand together now, they were licked! It was a showdown.

There was only one thing to do—take a referendum of the shareholders as to the basis on which they wished the year's business handled. The Board of Control of the Grain Growers' Grain Company therefore issued the following circular letter, which was mailed to every farmer shareholder:

"This matter we now bring to your notice is the most important yet."

"At a meeting of the Grain Exchange, held a few days ago, the Commission Rule was suspended for a year. This means that there is no fixed charge for handling grain, and any company or firm can, if they wish, handle car lots for nothing. How did this come about? The Elevator Companies did it with the aid of Bank Managers and other Winnipeg men outside of the Grain Trade, who hold seats on the Exchange, and voted with them. The intention of these Elevator Companies is to handle all grain for 1/2c. per bushel or for nothing in order to take it away from the Commission Men, who have no elevators, and especially to keep it away from the Grain Growers' Grain Company.

"The Elevator Companies can handle farmers' cars for nothing and still not lose anything. How? In four ways—

"1st. They all buy street grain and the immense profits they make on this will make up for any loss they have in handling cars for nothing."

"2nd. The dockage they get on street grain and on car lots passed through their elevators helps them."

"3rd. The charges on the cars loaded through their elevators helps them."

"4th. When they get your car it is sent to their own terminal elevator, and they earn the storage on it there which is very profitable."

"The commission man, such as ourselves, has none of these things to fall back on. His profit is what is left out of the cent a bushel commission after all expenses such as rent, taxes, insurance, wages for office help, telegrams, telephone, etc., are paid.

"The Elevator Combine know this. They know the weakness of the commission dealers' position and the strength of their own, and knowing it, deliberately cut out the commission and will offer to handle the farmers' grain for nothing in order to put the only opposition they have out of business. And mark you! this is aimed at our company more than any other, though we believe they are after all commission dealers. Some of them have said so. They want to kill us and they think they have at last found a way. Their dodge is simple. By handling cars for half a cent or nothing, they are going to bribe the farmers and our own shareholders to send cars away from us, and by keeping grain from us help to kill us and plant us that deep we shall never come up again.

"In this way they hope to 'rule the roost' and get back the good old days they had ten or twelve years ago."

"Can they succeed? It depends on the men who ship the grain. If they support the combine by giving the elevators (or the commission houses that work for the elevators under a different name) their cars, they may soon expect to find themselves in a worse position than they have ever been before.

"As a prominent commission man said the other day, 'The elevator companies are asking the farmers to help at their own funeral.' It is an anxious time for our own company. We have shown that with anything like fair play it may succeed. We have been growing stronger and, we believe, doing some good. Are our shareholders and friends going to take the bribe that is meant to put us out of business? We hope and believe not. For this reason we are taking a referendum vote of our shareholders."

It was at this crisis that the *Grain Growers' Guide* had an opportunity of demonstrating its value to the farmers as a fighting weapon. It seized the cudgels and waded right into the thick of the controversy without fear or favor. It came out flat-footed in its charges against the elevator interests and emphasized the warning of the Company in language that carried no double meaning.

"We have no quarrel with the Winnipeg Grain Exchange as an Exchange," said the *Guide*. "It is a convenience for gathering reports from other parts of the world, market conditions, and for drafting rules that facilitate and simplify business dealings.

"As we have often pointed out, however, the Exchange is being used by the Elevator Interests that seem to dominate it, to further their own particular ends with the result that the nefarious methods of the Elevator Trust bring suspicion and condemnation upon the Exchange and its members.

"The demand for the Royal Grain Commission arose from the methods pursued by the Elevator Companies in dealing with the farmers at country points. The pooling of receipts at country points is not forgotten by the farmers; heavy dockage and unfair grading and low prices paid when the farmers were compelled to sell and could not help themselves, are also not forgotten.

"Every injustice and disturbance in the trade that has taken place since grain commenced to be marketed in Manitoba, can be traced to the Elevator Monopoly."

"The farmers of this country owe nothing to the Elevator Trust and we have confidence enough in them to believe that they will not be bought over by them now. The Commission Men and Track Buyers certainly owe nothing to this trust either. They have helped in the past to carry the suspicion and sin arising from its methods and it commences to look as if they were getting tired of carrying the load."

Column after column of such plain talk was given place in the *Guide* week after week, together with reports of Grain

Exchange proceedings, interviews with commission men and elevator men, pronouncements of Grain Exchange officials and comment upon pamphlets circulated amongst the farmers by the North-West Grain Dealers' Association, etc. Everything having a bearing upon the situation was brought to light and analyzed. Letters from farmers throughout the country were published as fast as they reached the editor's desk, and they were coming pretty fast, about as fast as the mail could bring them.

They were reaching the office of the farmers' trading company by the bagful. The Company had asked three definite questions of the farmers in connection with the commission to be charged on grain shipped to the Company—whether or not the old rate should be maintained in spite of the action of the Exchange; whether the commission should be reduced; whether the whole matter should be left to the discretion of the directors. The letters poured in by the thousand and only two per cent. of the farmers recommended any reduction in the rates; of the remainder, seventy per cent. were in favor of the Company maintaining the one cent commission and the other twenty-eight per cent. were willing to abide by the decision of the directors.

The comments contained in some of these letters revealed strong feeling. Many farmers were ready to pay two cents commission per bushel if necessary, rather than sell to "the monopolies."

"I will pledge myself to ship every bushel of grain I grow to the Farmers' Company," wrote one, "even though the directors found it necessary to charge me five cents per bushel, coin."

"No, they cauna draw the blinds ower the daylights o' a

Scotchman," assured one old son of the heather. "I am verra pleased to leave the hale concern in your hands as I do believe you are thoroughly plumb and always square."

With this encouragement the directors announced that they would continue to charge a commission of one cent per bushel on wheat shipped to them, just as if the Commission Rule had not been suspended by the Exchange. Other commission merchants, they knew, intended to reduce their charges to half a cent per bushel; the elevator men, they expected, would handle the grain for the same and in many cases for nothing in order to persuade the farmers to ship their way. It would be a great temptation to many farmers who had been sitting on the fence, shouting "Sic 'em!" but never lifting a little finger to help, and it was to be expected that those with limited vision would ship their grain where they could make the biggest saving at the time.

Notwithstanding, the directors believed that the majority of the farmers would not prove one cent wise and many dollars foolish by failing to realize what the future might hold in store if the elevators succeeded in killing off competition. Finding that it was possible to handle oats on a smaller margin, they made the farmers a gift reduction of half a cent per bushel on oat shipments; otherwise the former rate was sustained.

The wheat ripened. Harvesting began. The long grain trains commenced to drag into Winnipeg across the miles of prairie. By the middle of September the weekly receipts of the farmers' company were running to 744 cars. In 1907 they had handled about five per cent. of the crop and seven and one-half per cent. of the 1908 crop; of the total number of cars so far inspected in this year of "free for all" methods, the Grain Growers' Grain Company handled about fifteen per cent.

Hopkins Moorhouse

When the end of the season brought the figures to a final total it was found that the farmers' organization had handled well over sixteen million bushels of farmers' grain. This was an increase over the preceding year of nearly nine million bushels, or 114 per cent. It was nearly one and one-half million bushels greater than all the previous years of operation and represented one-eighth of all the grain inspected during the year in Western Canada.

CHAPTER XIII

THE MYSTERIOUS MR. "OBSERVER"

Observation tells me that you have a little reddish mold adhering to your instep. . . . So much is observation. The rest is deduction.

—*Sherlock Holmes.*
Sign of Four (Doyle).

In Prehistoric Days, when one man hied himself from his cave to impress his ideas upon another the persuasion used took the form of a wallop on the head with a stone axe. It was the age of Individual Opinion. But as Man hewed his way upward along Time's tangled trails personal opinions began to jog along together in groups, creating Force. With the growth of populations and the invention of printing this power was called Public Opinion and experience soon taught the folly of ignoring it.

In the course of human aspiration Somebody who had a Bright Mind got the notion that in order to get his own way without fighting the crowd all he had to do was to educate the "Great Common Pee-pul" to his way of thinking and by sowing enough seed in public places up would come whatever kind of crop he wanted. Thus, by making Public

Hopkins Moorhouse

Opinion himself he would avoid the hazard of opposing it. The name of this Sagacious Pioneer of Special Privilege who manufactured the first carload of Public Opinion is lost to posterity; all that is known about him is that he was a close student of the Art of concealing Artifice by Artlessness and therefore wore gum rubbers on his feet and carried around a lot of Presents to give away.

It is quite possible to direct the thought of Tom-Dick-and-Harry. A skillful orator can swing a crowd from laughter to anger and back again. The politician who prepares a speech for a set occasion builds his periods for applause with every confidence. But it was to the public prints that they who sought the manufacture of Public Opinion were in the habit of turning.

There has always been something very convincing about "cold print." The little boy believes that the cow really did jump over the moon; for isn't it right there in the nursery book with a picture of her doing it? And despite the disillusionments of an accelerated age many readers still cherish an old-time faith in their favorite newspaper—a faith which is a relic of the days when the freedom of the press was a new and sacred heritage and the public bought the paper to learn what Joseph Howe, George Brown, Franklin, Greeley or Dana thought about things. This period gave place gradually to the great modern newspaper, the product in some cases of a publishing company so "limited" that it thought mostly in terms of dollars and cents and political preferments.

When the cub reporter rushed in to his city editor with eyes sparkling he cried out enthusiastically:

"Gee, I've got a peach of a story! Old John Smith's daughter's eloped with the chauffeur. She's a movie fan and—"

But it did not get into the paper for the very good reason that "Old John" was the proprietor of the big departmental store which took a full-page advertisement in every issue the year around. The editor would have used it soon enough, but—the business office—!

Then there was the theatrical press-agent, a regular caller with his advance notices and free electros of coming attractions, his press passes.

"Give us a chance, old man," he pleaded, perhaps laying down a good cigar. "Say, that was a rotten roast you handed us last week."

"Yes, and it was a rotten show!" the editor would retort. "I saw it myself."

The telephone rings, maybe—the business office again.

"The Blank Theatre have doubled their space with us, Charlie. Go easy on 'em for awhile, will you?"

The floor around the editor's desk was scuffed by the timid boots of the man who wanted his name kept out of the paper and the sure tread of the corporation representative who wanted his company's name mentioned on every possible occasion. Business interests, railway corporations, financial institutions—many of these had a regular department for the purpose of supplying "news" to the press. Some American railroads finally took to owning a string of papers outright, directly or indirectly, and one big Trust went so far as to control a telegraphic news service.

In fact, to such a pass did things come in the United States that the exploitation of the press became a menace to public interest and a law was passed, requiring every publication to register the name of its proprietor; in the case of corporate ownerships the names of the shareholders had to be filed and the actual owners of stock held in trust had to be named also. This information had to be printed in every issue and the penalties for suppression or falsification were drastic.

No such law was passed in Canada, although the reflection of the situation in the United States cast high lights and shadows across the northern boundary. Partizan politics were rife in Canada and too often have party "organs" and "subsidies" dampered down the fires of independence in the past. A few journals, however, even in the days before the great changes of the War, placed a jealous guard upon their absolute freedom from trammelling influences and to-day they reap the reward of public confidence.

While not a newspaper, the *Grain Growers' Guide* was a highly specialized journal for the Western farmer, aiming frankly at educating him to be the owner of his land, his produce, his self-respect and his franchise; to make him self-thinking and self-reliant and to defend him from unjust slurs.

The editorial responsibility of carrying out such a programme in the face of existing conditions required a well chosen staff. In Roderick McKenzie, then Secretary of the Manitoba Grain Growers' Association, the farmers had an editor upon whose viewpoint they could depend; for he was one of themselves. But lacking practical experience in newspaper work, it was necessary to secure an Associate Editor who would figure largely in the practical management of the publication. McKenzie was finding that his duties as Secretary of the Association were becoming too heavy for him to attempt editorial services as well; so that not long after the appointment of an Associate Editor he decided to devote his whole time to his official duties.

In its selection of a young man to take hold the *Guide* was fortunate. George Fisher Chipman was not only a very practical newspaper man to meet the immediate needs of the young journal, but he was capable of expanding rapidly with his opportunities. Well versed in the economic problems of the day, he was known already in many magazine offices as a reliable contributor upon current topics. He was well poised and, as legislative reporter for the *Manitoba Free Press*, Chipman had made something of a reputation for himself on both sides of the political fence as a man who endeavored to be fair and who upheld at all times the traditional honor of the press.

By training and inclination Chipman was in complete sympathy with the Farmers' Movement in Western Canada. Away east, in the Valley of Evangeline, near Grand Pre, Nova Scotia, he was brought up on a farm, learning the farmers' viewpoint as afterwards he came to know that of the big men in the cities. He believed in co-operation, his father having been a leader in every farmers' organization in Nova Scotia for more than twenty years.

It was not long before the young editor's influence made itself manifest in the official paper of the Western farmers. He saw many ways of improving it and organizing it for the widest possible service in its field. Editorially he believed in calling a spade a spade and, being free from political restrictions, Chipman did not hesitate to "get after" politicians of all stripes whenever their actions seemed to provide fit subject for criticism.

By the time the Commission Rule difficulty arose the *Guide* had increased its weekly circulation by many thousands. The new editor seized the opportunity for "active service" and waged an effective campaign. The Grain Exchange finally restored the One-Cent Commission Rule and never since has it been dropped.

Meanwhile, however, hostilities broke out anew in an unexpected direction. They took the form of "letters" to the press and they began to appear in five papers which were published in Winnipeg—two newspapers and three farm journals. Concealing his identity under the *nom-de-plume*, "Observer," the writer attacked the Grain Growers' Grain Company and the men at the head of it. Declaring himself to be a farmer, Mr. "Observer" endeavored to discredit the farmers' trading organization by casting suspicion upon its motives and methods of business. As letter followed letter it became evident that the object in view was to stir up discontent among the farmers with the way their own agency was being conducted.

After issuing a single, dignified and convincing refutation of these attacks, the Company ignored the anonymous enemy. But the gauntlet was picked up by the *Grain Growers' Guide*. It lay right at the editor's feet. Chipman recognized a direct challenge and did not propose to drop the matter with a denial in the columns of his paper—even with a dozen denials. His old reportorial instinct was aroused. Who was this mysterious "Observer"? Why was he going to so much trouble as to launch a systematic campaign? One thing was certain—he was NOT a farmer!

All good newspaper reporters have two qualifications well developed; they are able to recognize news values—having "a nose for news," it is called—and they are able to run down a "story" with the instinct of a detective. G. P. Chipman had been a good reporter—a good police reporter particularly. He had the detective's instinct and it did not take him long to recognize that he was facing a situation which could be uncovered only by detective work.

In the first place, he reasoned, the letters were too cleverly written—so cleverly, in fact, that they could be the product of a professional writer only, most likely a Winnipeg man. This narrowed the search at once. By process of elimination the list of possible "Observers" was soon reduced to a few names. It was an easy matter to verify the suspicion that the "letters" were paid for at advertising rates and the question uppermost became: "Who are the greatest beneficiaries of these attacks?"

"The elevator interests, of course!" was Chipman's answer to his own question. He began to make progress in his investigations and before long he became very much interested in an office which happened to be located in the Merchant's Bank Building, Winnipeg. Here a certain bright newspaper man with some farming experience had taken to business as a "Financial Agent"—telephone, stenographer and all the rest of the equipment.

So sure was Chipman that he was on the right track in following this clue that finally he shut the door of his private office and wrote up the whole story of the "deal" which he expected to have been made between certain elevator men and this clever editorial writer who knew so much about money that he had opened up a Financial Agency. With the whole "exposure" ready for publication and the photograph of the "suspect" handy in a drawer of the desk, Chipman asked the "Financial Agent" to call at the *Guide* office.

"Thought you might like to look over that copy before we use it," explained the editor casually when his visitor's pipe was going well. He handed the write-up across his desk. "I want to be fair and there might be something—"

There decidedly was!—a number of things, in fact! Not the least of them was the utter surprise of the pseudo Financial

Agent. He did not attempt to deny the truth of the statements made for publication.

According to the story which he told the editor of the *Guide*, it had been the original intention to have these "letters to the press" signed by leading elevator men themselves; but when it was decided to hire an expert press agent to mould public opinion in such a way as to offset the "onesidedness" of the farmers' movement, none of the elevator men cared to assume the publicity. The name, "Observer," would do just as well. A committee was organized to direct and supervise the work of the press agent and the chairman of this committee conducted the negotiations with the newspaper man who was to undertake the preparation of the "letters" and other material.

By the terms of his contract the press agent was to be paid in equal monthly instalments at the rate of $4,000 per year, with a contract for two years. For this he was to write letters which would turn public opinion against this Grain Growers' Grain Company, which was getting so much of the farmers' grain, and minimize the growth of sentiment in favor of government ownership of internal and terminal elevators. These communications he was to have published in the various papers of Winnipeg and the West. Such was the story.

The better to conceal the wires beneath this publicity campaign and the identity of the writer, Mr. "Observer" opened his office as a Financial Agency and became a subscriber to the *Grain Growers' Guide*—one paper, of course, which could not be approached for the purpose in view. It was necessary, nevertheless, to clip and file the *Guide* very carefully for reference; hence the subscription.

The space used by the "correspondence" was paid for at regular advertising rates. The advertising bill each week amounted to about $150. But one factor in the success of the plan had been overlooked—the influence of the *Guide*. No sooner had the official paper of the Grain Growers pointed out the situation to its readers and suggested that papers which accepted material antagonistic to the farmers' cause were no friends of the farmers—no sooner was this pointed out than letters began to arrive in batches at the offices of all the papers which were publishing the "Observer" attacks. Most of these letters cancelled subscriptions and so fast did they begin to come that one after another the papers refused to publish any more "Observations," paid for or not.

For unknown reasons it was decided to call off the attempt to create public opinion against government ownership of elevators and with the letters aimed at the farmers' trading activities being refused publication, the employers of "Observer" had no further work for him to do.

As they were still paying his interesting salary each month, they offered him $1,500 to tear up his contract, he said. But with more than a year and a half still to run—over $6,000 coming to him—Mr. "Observer" had a certain affection for that contract. Fifteen hundred dollars? Pooh, pooh! He would settle for—well, say So-Much.

"You're talking through your hat!" scoffed his employers in effect.

"It's a six-thousand-dollar hat!" smiled "Observer" pleasantly.

"Well, we won't pay any such lump sum as you say," virtually declared his employers, not so pleasantly.

"Just as you wish, gentlemen. I'll wait, then, and draw my salary—$333.33 1/3 every month, according to contract. I know you don't want me to sue for it; because we'd have to air the whole thing in the courts and there would be a lot of publicity. So we'll just let her toddle along and no hard feelings."

He got his money.

The alleged attempt of these elevator men, whether with or without the sanction of their associates, to make public opinion by means of the "Observer" letters began in the fall of 1909. It lasted but a few weeks.

CHAPTER XIV

THE INTERNAL ELEVATOR CAMPAIGN

What constitutes a state? . . .
Men who their duties know,
But know their rights, and knowing, dare maintain.

—*Sir William Jones.*
Ode after Alcaeus.

Now, about this Government Ownership of Elevators. The Grain Growers had had it in mind right along. The elevators were the contact points between the farmer and the marketing machinery; therefore if his fingers got pinched it was here that he bled. Complaints of injustice in the matter of weights, dockage, grades and prices colored the conversation of farmers in many parts of the country and, rightly or wrongly, many farmers were profoundly dissatisfied with existing conditions at initial elevators. These elevators provided the only avenue by which grain could be disposed of quickly if transportation facilities were not fully adequate. It seemed to the farmers, therefore, that the only way to avoid monopolistic abuses was for the provincial governments to own and operate a system of internal storage elevators and for the Dominion authorities to own and operate the terminals. The elevators, declared the farmers, should be a public utility and not in

Hopkins Moorhouse

private hands.

This feeling first found definite expression in a request by the Manitoba Grain Growers prior to the Manitoba elections in 1907. The Manitoba Government declined to act on the request of the Grain Growers alone, but called a conference of municipal reeves and others interested. This conference was held in June and urgently requested the Manitoba Government to acquire and operate a complete system of storage elevators throughout the province, as asked for by the Grain Growers. Nothing was done at the first session of the renewed government, however.

Meanwhile the Grain Growers were circularizing the three Prairie Provinces on the need for a government system of elevators and at the annual conventions of the organized farmers in Manitoba, Saskatchewan and Alberta in 1908 strong endorsement of the idea was made. An "Inter-Provincial Council of Grain Growers' and Farmers' Associations" [1] had been created, and this body urged the several executives to wait upon their respective governments and try to obtain definite action.

At the suggestion of Premier Roblin, of Manitoba, a conference of the three premiers was arranged through the Secretary of the Inter-Provincial Council. It was the hope of the farmers that this might lead to uniform legislation, introducing government ownership of the elevators, and that the three provincial governments would join in an appeal to the Dominion Government for co-operation. In each province the whole subject had been dealt with exhaustively in the text prepared by the Grain Growers—the conditions making a government system of elevators necessary, how it could be created and the practicability of its operation, the question of financing and the beneficial results that would follow. It was the idea of the farmers that the provinces would purchase existing storage houses at a fair valuation, issuing government bonds to finance the undertaking and build new elevators where needed.

The provincial Premiers met at Regina on May 4th, 1908, talked over the matter, then sent for George Langley, M.P.P., one of the directors of the Saskatchewan Grain Growers' Association who occupied a seat in the Saskatchewan Legislature. They appointed Mr. Langley as a sort of ambassador in their negotiations with the Grain Growers' representatives, sending him to the Inter-Provincial Council to present verbally a couple of alternative propositions—that the Railways should be asked to build loading elevators with storage bins or that the management of the elevators should be taken away from the present owners and profits limited while the farmers' organizations became responsible for grades, weights, etc.

Back came the Grain Growers with a document which repeated their former demands and amplified their argument. They claimed that they were entitled to what they were asking if only because the farmers formed the major part of the population and their demands could be granted without placing any tax upon the remainder of the people. They requested a conference with the three Premiers to go into the matter in detail.

Not until November 4th, 1908, did this conference take place in Regina. When they did get together the Premiers were not posted well enough on details to promise anything more definite than that they would consult their colleagues and make reply in due course.

It was the end of January, 1909, before the Inter-Provincial Council had an official reply. The Premiers pointed to grave and complicated questions which stood in the way of granting what the farmers were asking. Constitutional difficulties, financial difficulties, legislative difficulties—all were set forth in a lengthy and well written memorandum. The British North America Act would have to be amended to grant the provinces authority to create an absolute monopoly without which success would not be assured. In short, there was such a tangle of overlapping jurisdictions, public interest in trade and commerce, federal rights, railway rights and so on that the Premiers could not see their way clear at all in spite of their great desire to help the farmers at all times.

The Grain Growers passed the document to their legal adviser and R. A. Bonnar, K.C., gave them his opinion in writing. That opinion was very complete, very authoritative, and poked so many holes in the "constitutional difficulties" that the farmers could see their way much more clearly than the Premiers, to whom they made dignified rejoinder. They handed on the holes while they were at it in the hope that the heads of the three Provincial Governments could take a peek through the "difficulties" for themselves and see just how clear the way really was after all.

The Provincial Premiers, however, took the step which logically followed their reply to the farmers. Resolutions were introduced in the Alberta and Manitoba Legislatures that His Excellency the Governor-in-Council be memorialized in regard to the elevator question and asked to provide government ownership and operation or to have the necessary powers to deal with the matter conferred upon the provinces.

Thus things rode until December 14th, 1909, when the Committee on Agriculture in the Saskatchewan Legislative Assembly recommended the appointment of a commission to make searching enquiry into the subject of government control and operation of the internal elevators as asked for by the Saskatchewan Grain Growers' Association.

Two days later, at the annual convention of the Manitoba Grain Growers, Hon. George Coldwell announced for the Manitoba Government that they had accepted the principle of establishing a line of internal elevators as a public utility, owned by the public and operated for the public. So unexpectedly did this good news come that the farmers were amazed at their own success. They had fought for it long and earnestly and victory meant a very great deal; but it had seemed still beyond reach.

In the case of Manitoba it only remained now to get together and thresh out the details. A strong committee was appointed to conduct negotiations with the Government and there was prepared a memorandum of the plan which the farmers recommended the Government to follow. This was presented on January 5th, 1910.

The Government and the Grain Growers then each got ready a bill for consideration by the Legislature. Many conferences took place. The Government refused the farmers' bill and the farmers did not approve of the Government's proposals. While leaving full financial control in the hands of the Government, the Grain Growers demanded that the operation of the elevators be undertaken by an absolutely independent commission without any political affiliations whatsoever; it was provided also that no officer of the Grain Growers could act on this commission. The Government did not deem it wise to let control of the managing commission out of its hands. So negotiations were broken off.

The Manitoba Government now prepared a new bill, but did not remove the features to which the farmers were objecting. This bill was passed and the Government voted $50,000 for initial expenses and $2,000,000 for acquiring elevators. Beyond a weak protest from the North-West Grain Dealers' Association the elevator owners had not shown much excitement over the situation. While the Manitoba Grain Growers were not satisfied that the Government plan would work out successfully and therefore refused to assume responsibility in connection with it, they were ready nevertheless to lend their best co-operation to the Manitoba Elevator Commission when it got into action.

In the Province of Saskatchewan an altogether different plan was evolved in due course. The investigating commission, appointed February 28th, 1910, consisted of three well qualified men—George Langley, M.P.P.; F. W. Green, Secretary of the Saskatchewan Grain Growers' Association; Professor Robert Magill, of Dalhousie University, Nova Scotia, the latter acting as chairman. The commission held sittings at many points in Saskatchewan, taking evidence from a large number of farmers, went to Winnipeg to meet representatives of elevator companies, the Exchange and Government officials, and also visited several American cities. Their final report, consisting of 188 typewritten pages, was handed to the Saskatchewan Government on October 31st, 1910.

In addition to the comprehensive scheme outlined by the Saskatchewan Grain Growers many different suggestions were considered by the commission, such as government ownership and operation, state aided Farmers' Elevators, municipal elevators and various modifications of these plans. All, however, were discarded by the commission in favor of an experiment in co-operative ownership and management by the farmers themselves, assisted financially by the Provincial Government.

The scheme presented by the executive of the Saskatchewan Grain Growers' Association appeared to be unworkable because it overstepped mere public ownership and operation of initial elevators to include methods of sampling, grading before shipment, bank and government loans, features outside the power of a provincial legislature. The schemes of municipal and district elevators, while appealing to local loyalty for patronage, did not secure the farmers' direct pecuniary interest to make the elevators successful in the face of competition. As to the Manitoba plan, the commission were unanimous in advising against it in view of the financial risk and the disadvantages of political influences which would tend to make themselves felt.

Instead, therefore, of a plan aiming at ownership of initial elevators by the State and management by the Government of the day, the commission recommended ownership and management by the growers of grain. Such a co-operative scheme would aim equally well at removing initial storage from the ownership of companies interested in grain trading—would recognize as promptly the feeling of injustice in the minds of many farmers—would seek just as fully to create marketing conditions which would give the farmer satisfaction and confidence. While both the Manitoba scheme and the proposed co-operative scheme involved financial aid by the State, the commission saw reason to believe that with control and management in the hands of the farmers themselves many of the risks and limitations of other plans would be avoided.

It is to be noted that in reporting upon general conditions in the grain trade of Canada in 1910 the Saskatchewan Elevator Commission pointed out the great change which had taken place since 1900. One factor in this had been the construction of new transcontinental lines and thousands of miles of branch railway lines together with a great increase in car supply and a more efficient and cheaper system of transportation. Again, the use of loading-platforms had introduced real competition with the elevators, almost fifteen million bushels of the 1908-09 crop in Western Canada having been shipped direct by the farmers. The development of co-operation among the farmers through the Grain Growers' Associations had led to much advantageous legislation, while Farmers' Elevators and Public Weigh Scales had had a salutary effect at many shipping points. The organization of the Grain Growers' Grain Company as a farmers' own selling agency likewise had exerted a wide influence for good all over the West, enabling the farmers to obtain first-hand information about existing methods of dealing in grain. Finally, the protection afforded by the Manitoba Grain Act was not to be questioned; for while it was impossible to draft any Act which would prevent all the abuses alleged, it had been the means of providing many weapons of defence for the farmer and unfamiliarity with these provisions by individual farmers was scarcely to be blamed upon the Act itself.

The improvement in conditions, compared with earlier years, was recognized by most of the farmers appearing before the commission and many of them had no personal complaint to make in regard to weights, grades or prices. They were advocates of provincial ownership not so much on their own behalf as upon behalf of settlers in newer districts. The commission, therefore, while not saying that there were no cases of sharp practice or no grounds for dissatisfaction, were impressed by the fact that however powerless farmers had been in earlier days they were now in a very different position. The strong feeling which many farmers had against the line elevator companies was based upon experiences of rank injustice and bitter recollections of the past; for this the elevator people could blame nobody but themselves. But the factors enumerated undoubtedly had improved the situation from the farmers' standpoint and it only remained to strengthen these factors to give the farmer complete control in the matter of initial storage.

The commission were unanimous in recommending co-operative organization of the farmers as the probable solution of the situation in Saskatchewan. They suggested the enactment of special legislation to provide for the financing of the undertaking by the farmers themselves, assisted by a government loan. That is, the farmers surrounding a point where an elevator was needed would subscribe the total amount of capital necessary to build it, paying fifteen per cent. in cash, the crop acreage of the shareholders at that point to total not less than 2,000 acres for each 10,000 bushels capacity of the proposed elevator; these conditions fulfilled, the government would advance the remaining eighty-five per cent. of the subscribed capital in the form of a loan, repayable in twenty equal annual instalments of principal and interest, first mortgage security. The commission also suggested that the responsibility of preliminary organization be thrown upon the farmers themselves by appointing the executive of the Saskatchewan Grain Growers' Association as provisional directors of the new grain handling organization.

When the matter came before the Saskatchewan Legislature the annual convention of the Saskatchewan Association was being held at Regina and the farmers declared themselves ready to assume responsibility and go ahead. A bill was introduced by the Government, embodying the recommendations of the Commission, and the Act incorporating The Saskatchewan Co-Operative Elevator Company, Limited, was assented to on March 14th, 1911.

Because of the unusual financial arrangements with the Provincial Government the capital stock was not set at a fixed amount but left subject to change from time to time by the Government. In order to protect the credit of the Province the Government thus was able to control the amount of stock the company could issue and thereby the amount of money the Government might be called upon to advance for the construction or purchase of elevators. Shares were placed at $50 each, available for farmers only, and a limit was set upon individual holdings.

It was provided that each local unit would have a local board of management and appoint delegates to an annual meeting where a Central Board of Management would be elected. The company was empowered not only to own and operate elevators and buy and sell grain, but to own and operate lumber yards, deal in coal and other commodities and "do all things incidental to the production, storing and marketing of grain."

By June 16th, 1911, the Provisional Directors[1] were able to call the first annual meeting of the new organization, having fulfilled the requirement of the Act that twenty-five "locals" be first organized, and by July 6th—the date of the general meeting at Moose Jaw—an additional twenty-one "locals" were ready. Thus they were able to start with forty-six units, representing $405,050 capitalization with 8,101 shares held by 2,580 shareholders.

The newly-elected directors[2] proceeded forthwith to let contracts for forty new elevators, standard type of thirty and forty thousand bushels capacity with cleaning machinery and special bins. Six existing elevators were purchased.

The Grain Growers' Grain Company agreed to act as selling agents for this new baby sister and wide-spread interest became manifest as the Grain Growers took another step into commercial circles.

[1] See Appendix—Par. 8.

[2] See Appendix—Par. 12.

[3] See Appendix—Par. 12.

CHAPTER XV

CONCERNING THE TERMINALS

I have but one lamp by which my feet are guided; and that is the lamp of experience. I know no way of judging the future but by the past.

—Patrick Henry.

With the establishment of co-operative elevators for the storing of grain at interior points the farmers of Western Canada launched out upon the greatest experiment in co-operation this continent has seen. The success of these elevators, owned and controlled by the farmers themselves, in all probability would evolve the final phase of internal storage in connection with the Canadian grain fields.

Co-incident with their agitation for government ownership of elevators at country points, the farmers were urging upon the federal authorities the desirability of government control and operation of terminal storage facilities. It was not enough that the Provincial Governments of the Prairie Provinces should protect the farmers within their boundaries; for the terminal storage of grain was a part of the system and the farmers contended that corporation control of the terminals by grain dealers was leading to abuses and manipulations of the grain that were not in the best interests of the country.

Grateful as they were, therefore, for the efforts to improve early conditions by legislation, it was the opinion of the Grain Growers that these contraventions of the Grain Act would be prevented only by acquisition of the terminals by the Dominion Government. Mere legislation and supervision by the Government would not provide an effective remedy.

At the head of the lakes the grain passed out of the control of the transportation companies into the hands of the grain dealers; it was the only point in transit where it became subject to manipulation. With the exception of those owned by the C. P. R., the terminal elevators were operated by dealers, largely controlled by United States concerns and managed by experts from across the line. It was frequently charged that terminal operators forgot that they ought to be warehousemen solely and sought profits outside those of legitimate elevation and storage charges, although these authorized charges paid ample return on capital investment. The farmers wanted this temptation of handling and mixing grain at the terminals removed so that terminal operators could not tamper with the grain while it was in their custody. The claims of the Grain Growers that mixing was going on at Fort William and Port Arthur were based upon the report of the Royal Grain Commission which had investigated the grain trade in 1906-7.

The first definite step taken to lay these matters before the Dominion Government was in the winter of 1908 after the formation of the Inter-Provincial Council of Grain Growers' and Farmers' Associations. At a meeting of these represen- tatives of all the organized farmers it was decided to send delegates to Ottawa. When these gentlemen reached their destination in May, 1909, they found themselves face to face with a large and active group of grain men, railway officials and bankers who had gathered to take a hand in the interview with Sir Richard Cartwright, then Minister of Trade and Commerce. Beyond some concessions regarding special binning of grain, nothing came of this trip apparently, although the Western farmers were supported strongly by the Dominion Millers' Association.

A second memorandum was presented early in 1910 and the Grain Growers were granted a very respectful hearing by the Government; for, while the organized farmers represented but part of the farming constituency in the West, they had the sympathy of the entire farming community behind them in these requests. They went home, however, feeling the need of concentrating their energies on organization if they were to get actual action from politicians.

They had not much more than got home safely before something happened which proved their assertions that all was not as it should be down on the lake-front. Mr. C. C. Castle, Warehouse Commissioner, one day held in his hand some official reports from the Inspection Department concerning certain elevator concerns and compared the figures with the returns made to the authorities by these concerns themselves. He shook his head at the discrepancies and started an investigation. There were three companies involved and after full evidence was taken legally these three companies were prosecuted for returning untrue statements and in the Police Court at Winnipeg they were fined a total of $5,550 by the Magistrate.

The next thing was the drafting of a Grain Bill which aimed to improve certain matters. It was considered by the Senate and passed. It reached the House of Commons and Hon. Frank Oliver took it by the halter and led it about. Before anything could happen to it, however, and the judges get a chance to study its good and bad points, July (1911) came along and Parliament dissolved like a lump of sugar dropped into a cup of tea and in the hub-bubbles of a general election everything was *in statu quo*, as they say. And when the race was over and the Party Nags back in their stalls, lo! new tenants were taking their turn at sliding around on the polished Treasury Benches and having a sun bath!

The new Minister of Trade and Commerce was Hon. George E. Foster. He looked over the Grain Bill, passed his hand along its withers and patted it on the rump. Then he sat down and made a copy of it, idealizing it by injecting a few "betterments," then trotted it out for inspection with tail and mane plaited and bells on its patent-leather surcingle. He did not claim to be its real father—only its foster-father. He introduced it to the House with a very lucid review of the whole agitation for improvement in the Grain and Inspection Acts since "Johnny" Millar, of Indian Head, Saskatchewan, handed in the Royal Grain Commission report in 1907.

The new Government proposed to grant government control of terminal elevators only on a limited and experimental scale. They wanted to test out the principle by lease or construction of two or three terminals at the head of the lakes before undertaking the financial responsibility of handling the entire terminal system. Heretofore there had been government supervision merely; but now for an experiment there would be government operation as well while the management of the remaining terminals would have to be satisfactory to the Government.

"The demand of the West is that the grain should not be manipulated at the terminals," declared Mr. Foster. "It does not matter a pin as to how that is brought about so that the thing itself is accomplished."

The new bill provided for sample markets and the farmers

did not like this unless the Government acquired the terminals as had been requested. Owing to the grain blockade, due to car shortage, feeling was running high in the West and the farmers eyed the new legislation closely. They came upon a clause which startled them and in the row that followed it looked at one time as if the new Bill would be led to the boneyard and killed.

One of the proposals of the Government was the formation of a Board of Grain Commissioners with wide discretionary powers. They would be made responsible for the proper conduct of the entire grain trade and deal with all matters pertaining thereto. They were to have the absolute say-so in regard to car distribution and there was one clause that threatened this protection for which the Western farmers had fought so hard in earlier days.

At once consternation spread among the Grain Growers, their apprehensions based upon bitter experience. They protested vehemently. Letters, petitions and resolutions slid all over the official Government desks and delegations followed to Ottawa. Not the organized grain growers alone, but the whole Western farming element was up in arms.

Nevertheless, the new Grain Bill passed the House of Commons and browsed over to the Senate.

It was the farmers' last chance to stop it. R. McKenzie and J. S. Wood, of the Manitoba Grain Growers; J. A. Maharg and F. W. Green, of the Saskatchewan Grain Growers, and E. J. Fream, of the United Farmers of Alberta—these practical men figuratively took off their coats and waded in when they got in conference with Senate members. They preferred to see the whole bill killed unless the objectionable clause regarding car distribution were struck out; they saw the old-time elevator abuses again becoming possible and quite nullifying the many good features which the new legislation possessed.

The final upshot was that somewhat unexpectedly Hon. Senator Lougheed, leader in the Upper House, withdrew the offending clause on behalf of the Government, although the Government felt that the farmers were unduly excited.

The new Board of Grain Commissioners was appointed without delay and consisted of three men who understood Western conditions—W. D. Staples, of Treherne, Manitoba; Frank E. Gibbs, of Fort William, and Dr. Robert Magill, now Secretary of the Winnipeg Grain Exchange. Dr. Magill was made Chief Grain Commissioner, for he had rendered excellent services in the past and commanded the respect of the entire West.

The Board was not long in reaching the conclusion that if grain dealing companies were to be eliminated from the business of owning and operating terminal elevators, outright purchase and breaking of leases would be necessary. The companies refused to lease to the Government voluntarily on any terms which the Board could recommend. Some would not lease on any terms whatever, claiming that to lease their terminals would dislocate their whole system of interior elevators, involving a loss of capital which had been invested legitimately. Apart from this, the Board had its hands so full with other important things that expropriation and all that it involved would claim their whole time and energy to the neglect of other urgent matters.

Accordingly, the Grain Commissioners recommended that the Government meet the immediate need of increased terminal facilities at the head of the lakes by building a three-million-bushel elevator, thoroughly equipped for storing, cleaning, drying and handling grain and with provision for future extensions to a capacity of thirty million bushels. They also approved of the Grain Growers' Grain Company leasing one of the C. P. R. elevators. In this way both the Board and the Grain Growers would gain first-hand knowledge of terminal elevator conditions.

While formulating a policy for terminal elevators the Grain Commissioners considered the need for terminal storage in the interior as well as at the lakefront. The increase in the area of the grain fields, particularly in Alberta, was straining the transportation facilities to the limit and the construction of the Grand Trunk Pacific promised to open up still more acreage. Railway rolling stock, railway yard accommodations at Winnipeg and Fort William and elevator storage were not keeping pace with the annual volume of new grain. The Government Inspection Department was up to its eyes in grain, working night and day during the rush season, while lake and ocean tonnage likewise were inadequate. Even the eleven million bushels of extra storage capacity being built at the lake at the time the Board was considering the situation would soon fill and overflow. Congestion at eastern transfer houses or terminal points was threatening, water freight rates were up and the export market disturbed and there was no reserve of storage capacity in Western Canada to meet emergencies. In a wet season the drying plants at Fort William and Port Arthur were far from adequate. Delayed inspection returns and terminal outturns, due to the recurring car shortage, prevented the farmers from financing and widened the spread between street and track prices as the close of navigation approached.

Reviewing all this, the Grain Commissioners came to the conclusion that it was time to consider seriously the erection of Government terminal facilities nearer the grain fields. Especially in Alberta was the need great for inspection and terminal storage to be nearer the producer. It would relieve congestion, benefit the whole grain trade and provide for the future possibility of alternate shipping routes via Hudson Bay or the Panama Canal.

It was true that the Royal Grain Commission of 1906-7 had raised objections to interior terminals and inspection, such as the extra expense of handling, the extra loss to the grain in handling and re-handling, the possibility of the railways solving the car shortage problem, the difficulty of getting shippers to send their grain to such elevators and so forth. But the Board considered that, in view of other possible routes than the Eastern, these objections were not strong enough to balance the benefits. Accordingly they recommended the Government to take action, the elevators to be regarded as public terminals in which mixing of grades would be forbidden.

While the farmers in all three Prairie Provinces were busy with these vital matters, the Grain Growers' Grain Company meanwhile was wading along through all the difficult seasons of car shortage, expanding its usefulness and trying its best to give the maximum of service the while it was reaching out into the export field in an experimental way.

Then, in 1911, a situation arose unexpectedly that caused turmoil among the officers of the pioneer company and led to considerable anxiety among the Grain Growers all over the West. For, through an excess of zeal upon the part of an employee, the Grain Growers' Grain Company suddenly found itself dragged into the maelstrom of "The Pit." It was accused of trying to corner the oat market and was forced to fight for very life.

So that at last it looked indeed as if Chance had delivered the farmers into the hands of those who preferred to see them eliminated altogether from the market.

CHAPTER XVI

THE GRIP OF THE PIT

Now, infidel, I have thee on the hip!

—Merchant of Venice.

The visitors' gallery is an excellent vantage point from which to view the trading floor of the Exchange. It runs the full width of the south wall. The chairs entrenched behind the rail have acquired a slippery polish from the shiftings of countless occupants just as the wall behind has known the restless backs of onlookers who have stood for hours at a stretch.

It is here that the curious foregather—good people from every walk of life except the grain business. The tourist who is "just passing through your beautiful city" and has heard that Winnipeg has the largest primary wheat market in the world—the tourist drops in to see the sights. Friend Husband is there, pretending to be very bored by these things while fulfilling his promise to take Friend Wife "some day when there's something doing." Young girls who only know that bulls hate anything red and that bears hug people to death— they are there, thrilled by the prospect of what they are about to witness with but a very vague idea of what it will be. A dear old lady from the quiet eddies of some sheltered spot has been brought in by the rest of her party to see "goin's on" of which she does not approve because gambling is a well-known sin. She is somewhat reassured by noting a few seats away a man who wears the garb of a clergyman; presently he will take notes for his forthcoming sermon on "The Propinquity of Temptation and Its Relation to the Christian Life." The two young women who whisper together in the corner have been reading stockmarket stories in the magazines and they are wondering which of the traders, assembling on the floor below, will have his coat and collar torn off and which will break down and give vent to those "big, dry man-sobs" when his fortune is wrecked!

Not the least of the sights at the Grain Exchange is the Visitors' Gallery!

Two tanned farmers are discussing quotations and general conditions in a matter-of-fact way. War demands, the unfavorable United States Government report and rumors of black rust are making for a bullish condition. Cables are up and the market promises to be wild this morning. The gong will go in five minutes.

"The Pit" is out in the middle of the floor. There is an octagonal platform, raised a couple of feet from the floor level. In the centre of this platform three wide steps descend to floor level again; so that the traders standing on the different steps are able to see over one another's heads and note each other's bids. On the west side of the Pit is an elevated, built-in desk like those seen in court-rooms, somewhat resembling an old-fashioned pulpit; here three men sit throughout the session. One keeps his fingers on the switch-box which operates the big clock on the north wall where the fluctuations of the trading are flashed on a frosted dial in red-light figures. At his left sits a second man whose duty it is to record the bidding on an official form for the purpose. At the right is a telegraph operator who sends the record of the trading as it occurs to other big Exchanges— Minneapolis, Chicago, New York, etc.

The telegraphic report registers in several instruments attached to the big blackboard that occupies the entire north wall. Operators with chalk and chalk-brush in hand move about the platform at the base of this blackboard, catching the quotations from the clicking instruments and altering the figures on the board to keep pace with the changing information. A glance at this great blackboard will furnish the latest quotations on wheat, oats, barley, flax, corn, etc., the world over.

Ranged along the entire east wall are the clacking instruments of the various telegraph companies for the use of the brokers and firms trading on the Winnipeg Exchange. Telephone booths at the north, seats for friends of members on the west side, weather maps, etc., beneath the gallery— these complete the equipment of the big chamber.

The group about the Pit, waiting for the market to open, grows rapidly as 9.30 approaches. Members of the Exchange saunter in from the smoking-room, swap good-natured banter or confer earnestly with their representatives on the floor. In response to the megaphoned bellow of a call boy, individuals hurry to the telephone booths. Messengers shove about, looking for certain brokers. The market is very unsteady; it may go up or down. The men are clustering about the Pit now; most of them are in their shirt-sleeves and they are on tip-toe like sprinters who wait for the starter's pistol. Some of them have instructions to dump wheat on the market; some have been told to buy. Hundreds of thousands of bushels will change hands in the first few minutes. The market may go up or it may go—

Bang goes the gong! They're off! Above the red abbreviation, OCT., at the bottom of the big clock the blood-red figure 5 indicates the opening of the market at $1.45 even. With a mad swirl the trading begins in a roar of voices. A small forest of arms waves wildly above jostling bodies. Traders dive for each other, clutch each other and watch the clock. The red figure 5 has gone out and 7/8 has in turn vanished in favor of 5/8—1/2—3/8—4—(?) Instead of going up, she's falling fast. Before the market closes the price may rebound to $1.55. Somebody will make a "clean-up" to-day and many speculators will disappear; for margins are being wiped out every minute.

To the Gallery it is a pandemonium of noise, unintelligible in the volume of it that beats against the void of the high chamber. Only one shrill voice flings up out of the roar:

"Sell fifty Oc, sev'-eights!" He offers 50,000 bushels of wheat for October delivery at $1.43 7/8 per bushel. It's that fellow down there with the blazing red tie half way up his collar. He hits out with both hands at the air as he yells. A surge of buyers overwhelms him. They scribble notes upon their sales cards and go at it again.

Down there in the melee those men are thinking fast. With every flash of the clock the situation changes for many of them. Some pause, watching, listening; others who have been quiet till now suddenly break in with a bellow, seemingly on the point of punching the noses of the men with whom they are doing business. Lightning calculation; instantaneous decisions! "Use your discretion" many of them have been cautioned by their firms and they are using it. A moment's hesitation may cost a thousand dollars. Trading in the Pit is no child's play; rather is it a severe strain even upon those who know every trick, every firm and the character of its dealings, every trader and his individuality, his particular methods—who know every sign and its meaning, who can read the coming shout by the first movement of the lips. And always, in and out, are darting the telegraph messenger boys with yellow slips that cause upheavals.

"Why don't they take their time and do their trading more quietly and systematically?" ventures Friend Wife up in the gallery.

"And lose a cent a bushel while they're turning around, eh?" laughs Friend Husband. "On a hundred thousand bushels that'd only be a thousand dollars. Of course that's mere carfare!"

The dear old lady from the quiet eddies of Shelterville is shaking her head in disapprobation and communing with herself upon the iniquities of gambling.

"My, oh my! What won't men do for money! Jt-jt! Just look at 'em! Fightin' like that for money they ain't earnt! An' that nice lookin' young feller with the intelligent gold specs!—Dear me, it's enough to make a body sad!"

She could not know that but comparatively few of the traders below were representatives of brokerage firms which were trading on margins for speculating clients—that most of the traders were negotiating legitimate deals in futures for firms who actually had the grain for sale, for exporters who would take delivery of the actual wheat for shipment, for milling companies who would grind it into actual flour.

Because trading for delivery in future months affords opportunity for speculation, it is not to be condemned necessarily. It is the balance wheel which steadies the entire grain business. Even the speculating element is not without its uses at times and the layman who ventures to condemn This or

That out of hand will do well to make sure he understands what he is talking about; for the business of the grain dealer is so subject to varying conditions and so involved in its methods that it is one of the most difficult to be found in the commercial world.

Trading in futures finds birth in the very natural disinclination of Mr. Baker to buy his flour by the warehouseful. He does not want to provide storage for a year's supply, even if he could stand such a large bite out of his capital without losing his balance. So while the bakery man is anxious to order his flour in large quantities for future use, he is equally anxious to have it delivered only as he needs it, paying for it only as it reaches him—say, every three months.

Before contracting for the delivery of the flour on this basis Mr. Miller must look to his wheat supply on a similar basis of So-Much every So-Often and he, too, has an eye on storage and, like his friend the baker, he "needs the dough," as they say on the street, and he does not want to part with any more hard-working money than he can help. Accordingly he looks around for somebody who has wheat for sale and will sell it right now at a fixed price but defer delivery and payment to a future date. With the price of his wheat thus nailed down, Mr. Miller can set the future price on his flour to his customers, taking delivery and paying for the wheat as he requires it for filling his flour orders.

In the meantime where is the wheat? Out near the fields where it was grown, in country elevators perhaps, ready for transportation to market as the law of supply and demand dictates instead of the whole crop being dumped at once and smothering prices below the cost of production. Or perhaps it is in store at the terminal where Mr. Exporter can handle it. It will be seen that the mutual arrangement to buy and sell for future delivery simplifies matters for everybody in the grain trade.

The manner in which the legitimate trader in futures protects himself from price fluctuation is easily understood. While a deal in cash wheat would refer to a definite shipment as shown by warehouse receipts, a deal for future delivery is merely an obligation involving a given quantity of grain at a given time at a given price. Being merely a contract and not an actual shipment, the seller does not require to produce the grain immediately nor is the buyer required to hand over the purchase price when the trade is made. Thus it is possible to buy a thousand bushels to-day for October payment and sell a thousand bushels to-morrow for October delivery, cancelling the obligation. The trade can be balanced at any time before October 1st. Again, a thousand bushels of October wheat may be bought (or sold) to-day and the future switched to May 1st by the sale (or purchase) of a thousand bushels for May delivery.

Take the man with the blazing red tie half way up his collar, the man who this morning offered to sell fifty thousand bushels for October delivery at $1.43 7/8. Suppose that he represents a company with a line of elevators at country points. To his office at Winnipeg has come word from country representatives that fifty thousand bushels have been purchased for the company. At once he enters the Pit and sells fifty thousand bushels for delivery at a future date, thereby "hedging" the cash purchase out in the country. Once this future of fifty thousand is sold the company no longer is interested in market prices so far as this grain is concerned. If the market goes up, their cash grain is that much more valuable, offsetting the loss of an equal amount on the future delivery; if the price goes down, what is lost on the cash wheat will be gained on the future. So that the difference between the price paid for the grain at the country elevators and the price at which they sold "the hedge" is the only thing which need concern the grain company and it is here they must look for expenses and profits. This method of hedging enables a grain company to make purchases in the country on much smaller margins than was possible in the early days when the marketing machinery was less completely organized. It eliminates to the greatest extent the necessity of speculating to cover risks.

The speculator's opportunity comes in connection with the fluctuations of the market in deliveries. He merely bets that prices will go up or down, as the case may be. He is not dealing in actual wheat but in margins. He buys to-day through his broker, who has a seat on the Exchange, and deposits enough money to cover a fluctuation of say ten cents per bushel. If October wheat to-day is quoted at $1.45 his deposit will keep his purchase in good standing until the price has dropped to $1.35. He must put up a further deposit then or lose the amount he has risked already, the broker selling out his holding. If the speculator is on the right side of the market—if he has guessed that it will go up and it does go up—he can sell and pocket a profit of so-many-cents per bushel, according to the number of points the price has risen. If he has bet that the market will go down the situation merely is reversed.

The machinery for handling the huge volume of business transactions in a grain exchange must be complete and smooth running to the last detail, so designed that every contingency which may arise will be under control. For simplicity and efficiency in this connection the Winnipeg Grain Exchange occupies a unique position among the great exchanges of the American continent; in fact, it is a matter for wonder that its methods have not been copied elsewhere.

The Winnipeg Grain and Produce Exchange Clearing Association is a separate organization within the Exchange and to it belong all the Exchange members who deal largely in futures. Each day the market closes at 1.15 p.m. By two o'clock every firm trading on the floor must hand in a report sheet, showing every deal made that day by the firm—the quantity of wheat bought or sold, the firm with whom the trade was made, the price, etc. If on totalling the day's transactions it is found that they entail a loss, the firm must hand over a cheque to the Clearing House to cover the loss; if a gain in price is totalled the Clearing House will issue a cheque for it to the firm so gaining. Thus, if Jones & Brown have bought wheat at $1.39 and the market closes at $1.35 they lose four cents per bushel on their purchase and must settle the difference with the Clearing House. All differences between buyers and sellers must be settled each day and if the volume of trades has been heavy, the Clearing House staff work on their books—all night, if necessary—until everything has been cleared for next day's business. The firm which loses to-day may gain by to-morrow's trades, maintaining good average business health. Any private trading which may take place after official trading hours is known as "curb" trading.

The rules of the Clearing House are very strict. Any firm which fails to report by two o'clock is fined. The Clearing House assumes responsibility for all purchases and sales and, being actually liable, keeps close tab on every firm. Each firm has a certain credit on the books of the Clearing House, allotted impartially, according to its standing, and this credit forms the fixed basis of that firm's dealings. If its activities exhaust the line of credit, the Clearing House calls for "original margins" at once—a deposit of so-many cents per bushel for every bushel involved and for every point which the market drops. The amount per bushel called for is entirely at the discretion of the Clearing House authorities and if the quantity of grain reaches dangerous proportions the deposit required may be set so high that it becomes practically equivalent to cash purchase. To "corner the market" under these conditions would require unlimited credit with the Clearing House.

When Jones & Brown are "called" for deposit margins they drop everything and obey. They have just fifteen minutes to reach the bank with that cheque, have it "marked" and rushed to the Clearing House. If they fail to arrive with it the Manager of the Clearing House will step into their office and if there were any "hemming and hawing" Jones & Brown would be reported at once to the Secretary of the Exchange who would call a hurry-up meeting of the Exchange Council and Messrs. Jones & Brown would find themselves posted and all trades with them forbidden.

All clerical errors in regard to trades are checked up by the Clearing House and fines paid in for mistakes. Only a nominal charge is made for its services—enough to pay overhead expenses—but the fines have enabled the Clearing House to accumulate a large Reserve Fund which gives it financial stability to provide for all responsibilities should occasion arise through failure of any firm. All futures which have not been cancelled before delivery date are negotiated through the Clearing House and with its assistance the grain can be placed just where it should go and tremendous quantities of it are handled without a hitch and with the utmost despatch.

Excitement in the Pit is not always over wheat. It may be oats. It was Canadian Western Oats which became the storm centre in 1911 when the Grain Growers got into difficulty with the "bears." Traders who attempt to boost prices are known as "bulls"; those who are interested in depressing the market are "bears." A trader may be a bear to-day and a bull to-morrow; thus the opposing groups are constantly changing in make-up and the firm which was a chief opponent in yesterday's trading may be lined up alongside the day following, fighting with instead of against. It is all in the day's business and the strenuous competition on the floor, into which the uninitiated visitor reads all manner of animosity and open anger, is a very misleading barometer to the actual good feeling which prevails.

In recording what now took place in the Pit in connection with the farmers' commission agency it will be well to remember that the rest of the traders would have acted in the same way toward any firm which was fool enough to leave the opening for attack. It may be that as the thing developed some of those who were specially interested in the downfall of the farmers' organization seized the opportunity to ride the situation beyond the pale of business ethics and in their eagerness to be "in at the death" revealed special vindictiveness. But in view of the long struggle with this element it was only what the Grain Growers should have expected when they ran their heads deliberately into the noose.

The situation was this: Shortly after New Year's the export demand for Canadian Western Oats became heavy and it looked as if in Great Britain and all over Europe, where the oat crop had been small, there would continue to be a shortage of oats. In spite of this situation, however, no sooner was the proposed reciprocity agreement reached between the Canadian and United States governments of the day, on January 26th, than market prices began to go down.

The then Manager of the Grain Growers' Grain Company came to the conclusion that this price lowering was a local condition and that the export market for oats was too strong to justify it or sustain it.

"I'll just step into the market and buy some oats," said he. "Later on I'll sell for export at a satisfactory figure." Accordingly, one fine morning he went into the Pit and began to buy.

Hopkins Moorhouse

The Manager's motive in attempting to sustain the market may have been of the best; but it was the first time that such methods had been attempted by the Grain Growers—methods which were not at all in keeping with the avowed principles of the Company. The Board of Control had every confidence in their Manager and, although he was merely a salaried employee and not an executive officer, he had been given a pretty free hand in the conduct of the Company's operations. Apparently it did not occur to him that he should consult the Board before entering the market on a speculative basis. Had the Board known what he was about to do they would have vetoed it; but when they did discover what was afoot it was too late to prevent the situation. It developed very swiftly.

"The Grain Growers are up to the neck in May oats," was the whisper which passed about among the other traders. That was all that was necessary.

"Sell May oats! Sell May oats!"

On every side of the Pit they were being offered by thousands of bushels—five—twenty-five—fifty thousand! The idea was to load up the Grain Growers' Grain Company to the point where their line of credit with the Clearing House would become exhausted, after which every bushel would require a marginal deposit. Then when the Company could carry no further burden the Clearing House would be forced to dump back the oats onto the market, breaking it several cents per bushel. At this lower price the traders who had obligated themselves to make these big deliveries would buy back the necessary supply of oats at a profit and everything would resume the even tenor of its way—except the Grain Growers, of course. Their serviette would be folded. Their chair would be pushed back from the table! They would be *through*!

Up until now all the troubles of the farmers in marketing their own grain may be said to have come from sources outside themselves; but in the present instance they had nobody to blame but themselves for the predicament. It arose at a time, too, when the other grain dealers were beginning to recognize the farmers as a force in the grain market—a force which had come to stay. It was unfortunate, therefore, that just as they were beginning to acquire a standing as a solid and sensible business concern, the Grain Growers' Grain Company should find themselves driven into a corner, their backs to the wall, the focus of pointing fingers and gleeful grins.

The fact that a salaried employee, not an officer of the Company, had acted on his own initiative without the consent of the directors was no excuse for a reliable business concern to tender as such. The first question flung back at them naturally would be: "Then your 'Board of Control' doesn't control, eh?" For although the Board of Control did not know what their Manager was doing until it was too late to prevent it, they should have known. That is what they were there for— to protect the shareholders from managerial mistakes.

However, there they were. The only thing they could do was to fight it out to a finish in the Pit and, if they survived, to see that no similar mistakes occurred in the future.

All sorts of rumors were flying about the corridors of the Exchange, gathering momentum as they passed from lip to lip, swelling with the heat of the excitement until it was a general guess that the Grain Growers must be loaded with anywhere between five and eight million bushels of oats more than they had been able to sell.

It was only a guess, though, and a wild one. Many traders would have given a good round sum to know exactly how the farmers' company stood on the books of the Clearing

House. Only the Clearing House and the Company itself knew the true figures and the Clearing House officials were men of the highest integrity who dare not be approached for secret tips.

Thanks to the splendid export connection which had been built up in the Old Country and to the equally solid financial relations with the Home Bank, the farmers' agency was selling oats for export very rapidly. It began to look as if they would get out from under the threatening avalanche without much loss, if any.

The Company's old-time enemies apparently saw an opportunity to undermine its credit at this crisis; for attacks began to appear in print—accusations of speculation, of official negligence and so forth. If the Grain Growers could be prevented from paying for the large quantity of oats, delivery of which they would have to take on May 1st to complete the export sales made during the winter—if they could be made to fail in filling these export orders when navigation opened, they would be smashed.

But in attacking the credit of the Grain Growers, these opponents overlooked the rapid increase in paid-up capital and the ability of the farmers to secure money outside of Winnipeg. It was not being forgotten by the Grain Growers that upon the first day of May there would be delivered to them over 2,200,000 bushels of oats.

When the day arrived, therefore, the money was on hand to meet every contingency. Every bushel was paid for immediately. Within a few weeks half of the quantity was riding the waves of the Atlantic, bound for the Old Country to fill part of the sales already made there.

Before long some of the grain companies which had sold the

oats were trying to buy them back. Had the farmers' company been a speculating firm they might have turned upon the market and cornered the oats with a vengeance. It was one of those rare occasions when a corner could have been operated successfully to a golden, no-quarter finish; for the export demand was sustained and the local market could have been made to pay "through the nose" for its fun.

CHAPTER XVII

NEW FURROWS

Fishes, beasts and fowls are to eat each other, for they have no justice; but to men is given justice, which is for the best.

—Hesiod.

The situation was changing indeed for the Grain Growers in Western Canada. In spite of all opposition the farmers had made themselves a factor in the grain trade and had demonstrated their ability to conduct their affairs on sound business principles. Co-operative marketing of grain no longer was an untried idea, advocated by a small group of enthusiasts. The manner in which the farmers' pioneer trading agency had weathered the stormy conditions of its passage from the beginning and the dignified stand of its directors—these gradually were earning status in the solid circles of the business world.

Out in the country also things were different. Those farmers who at first had been most certain that the trading venture would crumble away like so many other organized business efforts of farmers in the past, now were ready to admit their error—to admit that a farmers' business organization, managed by farmers, could succeed in such ample measure that its future as a going concern was assured. Instead of hovering on the outskirts of its activities, like small boys surrounding a giant fire-cracker on Victoria Day—waiting for the loud bang so freely predicted—these gentlemen were beginning to look upon it as a safe investment.

The success of the Grain Growers' Grain Company was an argument for co-operation which could not be overlooked and the co-operative spirit spread rapidly among the farmers in many districts.

It will be remembered that the promoters of the grain company had intended originally to operate under a Dominion charter but were compelled by circumstances to content themselves with provincial powers. The farmers now were finding themselves too restricted and application was made for a new charter which would facilitate the transaction of business in other provinces than Manitoba. Special powers were asked for and by special Act of Parliament the charter was granted in 1911 in the face of considerable opposition at Ottawa from those whom the farmers regarded as representing the Canadian Manufacturers' Association and the Retail Merchants' Association.

For the trend of the organized farmers was quite apparent. No secret had been made of the views entertained by the Grain Growers regarding co-operation. To familiarize every member of the various organizations with the history of co-operative achievements in other countries had been the object of many articles in the *Grain Growers' Guide* and much speech-making from time to time. The possibility of purchasing farm supplies co-operatively in addition to co-operative marketing of grain was being urged convincingly. And during the long winter evenings when the farmer shoved another stick into the stove it was natural for him to ask himself questions while he stood in front of it and let the paring from another Ontario apple dangle into the ash-pan.

"The fellow who made that stove paid a profit to the Iron an' Steel Trust who supplied the raw iron ore," considered he. "Then he turned around an' added a profit of his own before he let the wholesaler have it. Then the wholesaler chalked up more profit before he shipped it along to Joe Green over in town an' Joe just naturally had to soak me something before I got her aboard for home. That's profits on the profits! It's a hot proposition an' it's my money that goes up the flue!"

When he added further profits which he figured might be due to agreements between supposed competitors in prices, the Grain Grower was quite ready to believe that he had paid about twice as much for that stove as the thing would cost him legitimately if he dealt with the maker direct. Here was the High Cost of Living that everybody was talking about. The remedy? The same chance as the Other Fellow for the farmer to use the resources of Nature and, by co-operation, the reduction to a minimum of production and distribution cost.

"I've done it with my grain. Why can't I do it with what I need to buy?" That was what the Grain Grower was asking himself. "Why must I feed and clothe and buy the smokes for so many of these middlemen?"

So when the directors of the grain-trading company came before him with the suggestion of buying a timber limit in British Columbia in order to put in their own saw-mills eventually to supply building materials on the prairie, the Grain Grower slapped his leg and said: "Good boy! An' say, what about a coal mine, too?"

That was the beginning of great developments for the organized farmers of Western Canada. It was the beginning of new furrows—the opening up of new vistas of emancipation, as the farmer saw it. And as the furrows lengthened and multiplied they were destined to cause much heart-burning and antagonism in new directions.

The timber limit which the Grain Growers' Grain Company purchased was estimated to contain two hundred and twenty-two million feet of lumber. A Co-Operative Department was opened with the manufacture and sale of more than 130 carloads of flour at a saving to the farmer of fifty cents per cwt, even this small beginning registering a drop in milling company prices. Next they got in touch with the Ontario Fruit Growers' Association and sold over 4,000 bbls. of apples to Western farmers at the Eastern growers' carload-lot price, plus freight, plus a commission of ten cents per barrel. More than one hundred carloads of coal were handled in one month and the farmers then got after the lumber manufacturers for lumber by the carload at a saving of several dollars per thousand feet.

Still experimenting, the Grain Growers' Grain Company added to the list of commodities in 1912-13—fence posts, woven fence wire, barbed wire and binder twine. Followed other staples—cement, plaster, sash and doors, hardware and other builders' supplies; sheet metal roofing and siding, shingles, curbing, culverts, portable granaries, etc.; oil, salt and other miscellaneous supplies; finally, in 1914-15, farm machinery of all kinds, scales, cream separators, sewing machines and even typewriters. Of binder twine alone nearly seven million pounds was handled during this season. Thus did co-operative purchasing by the farmers pass from experiment to a permanent place in their activities.

Expansion was taking place in other directions also. In 1912 the Company leased from the Canadian Pacific Railway a terminal elevator at Fort William, capacity 2,500,000 bushels. A small cleaning elevator was acquired at the same place and, with an eye to possible developments at the Pacific Coast, a controlling interest in a small terminal elevator in British Columbia was purchased. At Port Arthur, on a six-hundred-foot lake frontage, a new elevator has just been built with a storage capacity of 600,000 bushels.

So much for terminal facilities of this farmers' pioneer trading organization. Now, what about the country elevators for government control of which the farmers had campaigned so vigorously in the three Prairie Provinces? As we have seen, the problem had been handled in Saskatchewan along very different lines to the method adopted in Manitoba. In Manitoba the 374 elevators, owned by the Provincial Government and operated by the Provincial Elevator Commission, showed a loss. It was even hinted in some quarters that the Manitoba Government had no intention in the first place of operating at anything but a loss. Whether or not there was any ground for these irreverent suspicions, the fact remained that the Government elevator system in Manitoba was beginning to assume the bulk of a snow-white elephant. The Government, not entering the field as buyers, had tried to run the elevators as a storage proposition solely. In 1910-11 the loss had exceeded $84,000 and the year following was not much better. At last the Government said in effect to the Grain Growers:

"We've lost money on this proposition. We tried it out to please you farmers, but you're still dissatisfied. Try to run 'em yourselves!"

"We'll just do that," replied the farmers, although the Grain Growers' Grain Company was not enthusiastic over the prospect of converting the elevator failure into immediate financial success.

It was too much to expect. At many points the Government owned all the elevators in sight. In some places there was too much elevator accommodation for the district's volume of business. In certain cases the elevators which had been sold to the Government were practically discards to begin with. However, the need for improvement in the service which the farmers were getting at country points was so very great that finally, in 1912, the farmers assumed control of the government system in Manitoba.

It was late in August when this came about. With only three or four weeks in which to prepare for the season's crop, make repairs, secure competent managers, travelling superintendents and office staff the results of the first season scarcely could offer a fair test. Even so, prices for street grain went up at competing points. Line elevator companies began asking the farmer for his grain instead of merely permitting him to place it in their elevators.

The farmers were quick to note this and asked that the elevator service be continued by their company. With better organization the following season brought still greater improvement in service. Prices rose. The special binning service from their own elevators the farmers found genuine, not just a last-minute privilege granted to secure their grain. In spite of bad crop conditions in 1914-15, the elevators continued to succeed under the farmers' own management and, the year following, letters of highest praise from farmers everywhere marked the complete success of the undertaking. So excellent was the service now being rendered by the Company that independent Farmers' Elevators in several instances approached the Grain Growers and sought their management.

The handling of co-operative supplies at elevator points began in 1913-14. Flour houses were erected where prices were out of proportion and at other places the elevator agents began to arrange for carload shipments and proper distribution of coal among the farmers at a saving of from two to three dollars per ton.

These co-operative lines at elevator points soon were enlarged with much success. In addition to the elevators leased from the Manitoba Government the Grain Growers' Grain Company bought outright, erected or leased sixty elevators of its own.

Those who were watching all this steadily grew more restive. The Farmers' Movement in the West was fast becoming a subject of bitter debate.

"When farmers advance to the last furrow of plowed land on the farm they breast the fence which skirts the Public Highway," argued many Men of Business. "They are climbing over the fence!"

But the organized farmers were not inclined to recognize fences in restriction of honest competition. They believed they were on the Open Range and held unswervingly on their way.

CHAPTER XVIII

A FINAL TEST

We sometimes had those little rubs which Providence sends to enhance the value of its favors.

—Vicar of Wakefield.

While developing co-operative purchasing of farm supplies the pioneer business organization of the farmers had continued its policy of expansion in the grain business. The ideal of the farmers had been to reduce to the lowest possible point the cost between the producer in Western Canada and the Old Country consumer who bought most of the Western grain. By engaging in the export business they hoped to become an influence in keeping export values—the price at Port William, in other words—at a truer level.

Prior to 1912 the export activities of the Grain Growers had been restricted necessarily to an experimental basis; but on January 1st, 1912, the "Grain Growers' Export Company," as it was called, was organized for business on a larger scale.

It now becomes necessary to record a final test of the Grain Growers' Grain Company inasmuch as it demonstrated the mettle of the farmers in a significant manner—the test of serious internal disagreement. Of all the threatening situations through which this organization had passed none was more critical than this later development.

The trouble was a brew which simmered for some time before the steam of it permeated beyond directors' meetings. It began early in 1912 as an aftermath of the unfortunate deal in oats, bubbled along to a boil with the fat finally in the fire at the annual meeting of the shareholders. The consequences were ladled out during 1913 and the bill was settled in full at the annual meeting that year with a cheque for nearly a quarter of a million dollars.

Like most internal troubles in business organizations the personal equation entered into it. Certain of the directors were inclined to criticise other directors and to be somewhat dictatory as to how the farmers' business should be conducted. With the idea of improving the system of management, the directors at this stage abolished the Board of Control and the President was made Managing-Director with supervisory and disciplinary powers.

Not long after this, at a special meeting of the directors to consider future management, four of the nine directors introduced a resolution to declare the position of Managing-Director vacant. They failed to carry it—and promptly resigned.

This occurred in March. In the June columns of the *Guide* these four directors addressed an open letter to the share-holders, urging full representation at the forthcoming annual meeting in order that their criticisms might be threshed out. President Crerar joined in the request for a full meeting of shareholders. If the loyalty or ability of any director was to be questioned because he refused to surrender his judgment to other directors who might disagree with him on certain matters, it was time to have an understanding. So far as he was concerned, he could not agree to become a mere speaking-tube for others who might want their own way against his own convictions of what was in the best interests of the farmers.

When the annual meeting opened, on July 16th, there was a record attendance of shareholders and during the routine preliminaries it was evident that expectancy was on tip-toe among the farmers. The split in the directorate was a vital matter.

In delivering his annual address the President detailed the business of the organization for the past year, referring but briefly to the facts which had led up to the resignation of the four directors. The Shareholders' Auditor followed with the balance sheet, giving detailed accounts of receipts, expenditures, assets and liabilities; he answered all questions asked. Then came a resolution, expressing the thanks of the shareholders to the President—and this moment was chosen by the leader of the revolt to spin his pin-wheels.

The debate began at three o'clock in the afternoon. It did not end until ten at night. The President retired from the chair and the Auditor was called on for detailed information, covering a period of several years past. In the long speech which was then made by the leader of the critics the President was declared responsible for all the alleged mismanagement and his retention in office undesirable.

To the surprise of everyone a fifth director now took the floor and joined the attack. Not having been one of the four directors who resigned, this new criticism was unexpected and the tension of the meeting grew. After amusing himself and the audience for awhile with a humorous speech, No. 5 ended by suggesting that the President was not sufficiently wicked to be driven from office.

Arose the remaining three members of the resigning quartette and, one after another, had their say. Finally, when words failed them and they rested their case, the President spoke briefly.

In the annual address, which he had delivered that morning, no attempt had been made to deny the inadequacy of the Company's office organization to cope with the exceptional crop conditions of 1911 and 1912. The latter season particularly had been very trying owing to the lateness of the crop and the wet harvesting conditions. Twenty-five per cent. of the grain, which started for market a month late, was tough, damp or wet. The arrival of snow had prevented hundreds of thousands of acres from being threshed and, on top of it all, railway traffic had become congested so that cars of grain got lost for weeks and even months and there were long delays in getting the outturns of cars after they were unloaded. Money was scarce and farmers who were being pressed for liabilities to merchants, banks and machinery companies found it hard to get cars; naturally, once they had shipped, they were in no mood for further delays.

Owing to the condition of the grain, too, the grading was so uncertain that exceptional care had been necessary in accepting bank drafts on carloads of grain for amounts nearly double their possible value under the unusual current crop conditions. Even with the greatest care the Company found that in many instances they had given greater advances than were realized when the cars were sold. The refusal of drafts, passed by some local banks for amounts the managers should have known could not be met, led to many hard things being said against the farmers' agency.

Under these conditions it was only to be expected that the work in the office would become congested badly for weeks at a stretch. Double the amount of work was entailed in handling a given quantity of grain, compared to the season before. The Company was handicapped for office space also and errors were bound to occur in a business involving so much detail that a simple mistake might lead to infinite trouble. Correspondence had not been answered as promptly as it should have been, the necessary information regarding shipments being unavailable.

All of these things had been met frankly in the President's annual address and now when he brought the day's animated debate to a close he added merely a word or two regarding the strong financial position to which the farmers' pioneer trading organization had won its way in the commercial world. He pointed out the future that lay before it. Upon personal attacks he did not comment at all.

Immediately a unanimous vote of thanks for his untiring work and loyalty was tendered Mr. Crerar. The debate was over. The following morning the officers for the ensuing year were chosen and only one of the four directors who had resigned from the old Board was re-elected. He withdrew and the whole incident was closed.

But the real test was yet to come. The withdrawal of the four directors had left but five to cope with the difficult situation of the Export Company. It had found itself with a large amount of ocean freight on its hands—freight which had been secured on favorable terms from shipping agents for use later in transporting grain which the farmers' agency expected to sell in the Old Country. It was decided to cut off the export business entirely for the time being and to re-let the ocean shipping space to other exporters. The price of ocean freight fluctuated to such an extent, however, that rather than accept an immediate loss it was thought better to use the freight, after all, making shipment to fill.

At the time of the sixth annual meeting the Export Company had stood about level on the books; but during the two succeeding months the grain shipped from Fort William went out of condition while crossing the ocean and when it arrived in port the Old Country buyers refused to look at it. Heavy charges had to be met in treating to bring it to sale condition and very heavy losses were incurred. Before the matter was cleaned up finally these losses totalled more than $230,000.

When a quarter of a million dollars has been expended in a direction where tangible results have not been in evidence—when it has been sacrificed apparently for the sake of a principle—then does the manner in which such a loss is accepted become significant. The exporting of grain had begun to receive particular attention from the shareholders of the Grain Growers' Grain Company following the season of 1907-8 when they discovered the apparent margin of profit in the export business during much of the season to be from eight to twelve cents per bushel. This had been due, no doubt, to the fact that it was a time of financial stringency and only a few exporting firms could get the money necessary to carry on the business. The export value of grain, the farmers had figured, should be its value in the world's markets, less the cost of delivering it. By engaging in the export business, obtaining their cable offers regularly from the Old Country, they felt that their competition would be a factor in governing the prices paid the farmer, thereby benefiting every farmer in the West.

That this had been accomplished the shareholders of the trading company were convinced. Therefore, instead of losing their heads as well as this large sum of money, they examined the situation coolly and sanely, making up their minds that the loss was due to the grain going out of condition because of the unusual weather which had characterized the season. No doubt the executive and directors had been handicapped by their lack of knowledge as to the methods and manner in which the export business was done; but that was to be expected and only by experience could they learn.

"Can the export part of our business be developed successfully with a little more time?" asked the farmers.

"Yes, we believe so," replied their officers.

"That's all we want to know. Write a cheque to cover this loss, reorganize the Export Company and stick to it."

This faith in their officers, in themselves and in the cause they had at heart was justified within the next two seasons when success was achieved with the subsidiary concern and the farmers were able to congratulate themselves that they had been sufficiently level-headed not to allow themselves to be stampeded from the exporting field altogether to the great weakening of their influence.

The accomplishments of the Grain Growers in marketing their own grain cannot be dismissed with careless gesture. Their severest critic must admit that the manner in which the farmers conducted themselves in the face of the situation that threatened entitles them to respect.

CHAPTER XIX

MEANWHILE, IN SASKATCHEWAN—

An old man on the point of death summoned his sons around him to give them some parting advice. He ordered his servants to bring in a faggot of sticks, and said to his eldest son: Break it. The son strained and strained, but with all his efforts was unable to break the bundle. The other sons also tried, but none of them was successful. Untie the faggots, said the father, and each of you take a stick. When they had done so, he called out to them: Now break; and each stick was easily broken. You see my meaning, said their father. Let affection bind you to one another. Together you are strong; separated you are weak.

—Aesop.

Eventful years, these through which the Grain Growers of Western Canada were passing. While the Grain Growers' Grain Company was undertaking the initial experiments in co-operative purchasing of farm supplies, showing the Manitoba Government that farmers could run elevators satisfactorily and fighting its way forward to success in the exporting field, how were things getting along in Saskatchewan? With $52,000 and another four or five hundred in loose change tucked away in its hip pocket as the net profit of its first season's operations the new system of co-operative elevators had struck out "on a bee line" for Success and was swinging along at a steady gait, full of confidence. The volume of business handled through these elevators the first year had been affected by the failure of the contractors to finish construction of all the elevators by the dates specified. Even so, the new company had handled 3,261,000 bushels of grain, more than half of it being special binned.

In planning to build eighty-eight new elevators in 1912 and to purchase six, thereby bringing the total to 140 co-operative elevators, the directors thought it wise to form a construction department of their own instead of relying upon outside contractors. Also it was decided to open a commission department of their own at Winnipeg, the volume of business in sight being very encouraging. This move was not made, however, because of any dissatisfaction with the Grain Growers' Grain Company's services as selling agent; on the other hand, although crop conditions had been perhaps the most unfavorable in the history of Saskatchewan and the grain with its diversity of grades therefore very difficult to market satisfactorily, the Board of Directors acknowledged in their annual report that the wisdom of the arrangement with the Grain Growers' Grain Company had been proved by the satisfactory working of it.

The volume of business handled by the 137 elevators in operation the second year jumped to 12,900,000 bushels with a net profit of approximately $168,000, and it was apparent that the general acceptance of the co-operative scheme throughout the province would mean organization upon a large scale. This was emphasized during the 1913 grain season when 192 elevators were in operation and about 19,500,000 bushels of grain were hauled in to the co-operative elevators by farmers.

This rapid expansion of the Saskatchewan Co-Operative Elevator Company was entailing such an increase in staff organization that it became necessary to provide special office accommodation. Accordingly a site for a permanent building of their own was purchased in 1914 at Regina and the following year a modern, fireproof building was erected. It stands two storeys on a high basement, with provision for additional storeys, occupies a space of 9,375 square feet, has interior finish of oak and architecturally it is a matter of pride to the farmers who own it. This building has become the headquarters of the Saskatchewan Co-Operative Elevator Company and likewise the Saskatchewan Grain Growers' Association, the offices of the latter occupying the entire top floor.

While the erection of this building afforded visible proof of financial progress the Saskatchewan farmers were warned by the directors and the general manager of the "Co-Op" that co-operation which was allowed to degenerate into mere production of dividends would but reproduce in another form the evil it was intended to destroy. The ideal of service was the vital force which must be kept in mind and the work of the Grain Growers' Association in fostering this ideal must be encouraged.

"The Association has its great work of organization, education and agitation," stated Charles A. Dunning, the elevator company's manager, "and the company the equally great work of giving practical effect to the commercial and co-operative ideals of the Association, both institutions being branches of one united Farmers' Movement having for its object the social and economic uplift of the farming industry."

Not a little of the early success of the Saskatchewan Co-Operative Elevator Company was due to the energy and business ability which Dunning brought to bear upon its organization and development. The story of this young homesteader's rise from the ranks of the Grain Growers is worth noting. It was back in 1902 that he first reached the West—a seventeen-year-old Englishman, "green" as the grass that grew over there in Leicester. He did not know anything then about the historic meeting of pioneer grain growers which Motherwell and Dayman had assembled not long before at Indian Head. He was concerned chiefly with finding work on a farm somewhere and hired out near Yorkton, Saskatchewan, for ten dollars a month. After awhile he secured one of the Government's 160-acre slices of homestead land and proceeded to demonstrate that oxen could haul wheat twenty-five miles to a railway if their driver sat long enough on the load.

There came a day when Dunning, filled with a new feeling of independence, started for Yorkton with a load of wheat and oats. It was along towards spring when the snow was just starting to go and at a narrow place in the trail, as luck would have it, he met a farmer returning from town with an empty sleigh. In trying to pass the other fellow Dunning's sleigh upset. While helping to reload the farmer imparted the information that oats were selling for eight cents and all he had been able to get for his wheat was something like thirteen cents in Yorkton the day before! The young Englishman's new feeling of "independence" slid into his shoe-packs as he stared speechless at his neighbor. Right-about went his oxen and back home he hauled his load, angry and dismayed and realizing that something was wrong with Western conditions that could bring about such treatment.

When a branch of the Grain Growers' Association was formed at Beaverdale, not far from his homestead, it is scarcely necessary to say that young Dunning joined and took an active part in the debates. Finally he was chosen as

Hopkins Moorhouse

delegate for the district at the annual Grain Growers' convention at Prince Albert on condition that he could finance the trip on $17.50. The story is told that Dunning figured by making friends with the furnace man of one of the hotels he might be allowed to sleep in the cellar for the week he would be in Prince Albert and manage to get through on this meagre expense fund! At any rate he did find a place to lay his head and, if reports be true, actually came back with money in his pocket.

It was at this convention that the young man first attracted attention. The delegates had deadlocked over a discussion in regard to a scheme for insuring crops against hailstorms in Saskatchewan, half of them favoring it and half opposing it. The young homesteader from Beaverdale got up, ran his fingers through his pompadour and outlined the possibilities of co-operative insurance which would apply only to municipalities where a majority of the farmers favored the idea. He talked so convincingly and sanely that the convention elected him as a director of the Association and later when the co-operative elevator scheme was broached he was elected vice-president of the Association and the suggestion was made that he undertake the work of organizing the new elevator concern. Incidentally, the man who suggested this was E. A. Partridge, of Sintaluta—the same Partridge who had fathered the Grain Growers' Grain Company and who already had located T. A. Crerar, of Russell, Manitoba.

Out of Dunning's suggestion at Prince Albert grew the Saskatchewan Hail Insurance Commission which was recommended to the Provincial Government by the Association in 1911 and brought into operation the following year. The legislation provided for municipal co-operative hail insurance on the principle of a provincial tax made operative by local option. Twenty-five or more rural municipalities having agreed to join to insure against hail the crops within the municipalities, authority would be granted to collect a special tax—not to exceed four cents per acre—on all land in the municipalities concerned. Administration would be in the hands of the Hail Insurance Commission, which would set the rate of the special tax. All claims and expenses would be paid from the pooled fund and all crops in the respective municipalities would be insured automatically. If damage by hail occurred insurance would be paid at the rate of five dollars per acre when crop was destroyed completely and *pro rata* if only partially destroyed. This co-operative insurance scheme was instituted successfully in the fall of 1912, soon spread throughout Saskatchewan and was destined eventually to carry more than twenty-five million dollars of hail insurance.

Shortly after the launching of co-operative hail insurance the discussions among the Saskatchewan farmers in regard to the co-operative purchasing of farm commodities for their own use came to a head in a request to the Provincial Government for the widening of charter powers in order that the Association might organize a co-operative trading department. In 1913 authorization to act as a marketing and purchasing agent for registered co-operative associations was granted and next year the privilege was extended to include local grain growers' associations.

Thus the Trading Department of the Saskatchewan Grain Growers' Association takes the form of a Central Office, or wholesale body, through which all the Locals can act collectively in dealing with miners, millers, manufacturers, etc. The Central sells to organized Locals only, they in turn selling to their members. The surplus earnings of the Central are distributed to the Locals which have invested capital in their Central, such distribution being made in proportion to the amount of business done with the Central by the respective Locals.

Hopkins Moorhouse

During its first season of co-operative purchasing the Association handled 25,000 tons of coal and in a year or two there was turned over in a season enough binder twine to bind fifty million bushels of grain—about 4,500,000 pounds of twine. When the Western potato crop failed in 1915 the Association imported four and one-half million bushels of potatoes for its members, cutting the market price in some cases a dollar per bushel. Flour, apples, cord-wood, building supplies, vegetables and groceries likewise were purchased and distributed co-operatively. The savings effected by the farmers cannot be tallied alone from actual quantities of goods thus purchased through their own organization but must include a large aggregate saving due to reduction of prices by outside dealers.

Such commodities as coal and flour being best distributed through local warehouses, it is likely that eventually the Saskatchewan Co-Operative Elevator Company will take a hand in helping the Association and the Locals with the handling of co-operative supplies by furnishing the large capital investment needed to establish these warehouses.

The necessary financial strength to accomplish this is readily conceived to be available after a glance at later developments in Saskatchewan. The co-operative elevators now exceed 300. The figures for the season of 1915-16 show a total of more than 39,000,000 bushels of grain handled with an additional 4,109,000 bushels shipped over the loading platforms. Without deducting war-tax the total profit earned by the Saskatchewan company within the year was in the neighborhood of three-quarters of a million dollars. The Saskatchewan Co-Operative Elevator Company in 1916 began building its own terminal elevator at Port Arthur with a capacity of 2,500,000 bushels. By this time there were 18,000 shareholders with a subscribed capital of $3,358,900, of which $876,000 was paid up.

In these later years a remarkable development is recorded also by the Saskatchewan Grain Growers' Association until it is by far the largest and best organized secular body in the province with over 1,300 Locals and a membership exceeding 28,000.

The Secretary of the Association—J. B. Musselman, himself a farmer—has done much hard work in office and looks forward to the time when the Locals will own their own breeding stock, assemble and fatten their own poultry, handle and ship their eggs, operate their own co-operative laundries and bakeries, kill and cure meat in co-operative butcher-shops for their own use—have meeting places, rest rooms, town offices, libraries, moving-pictures and phonographs with which to entertain and inform themselves. To stand with a hand on the hilt of such a dream is to visualize a revolution in farm and community life—such a revolution as would switch much attraction from city to country.

Whatever the future may hold in store, the fact remains that already much valuable legislation has been secured from the Government of Saskatchewan by the farmers. Perhaps in no other province are the Grain Growers in as close touch with the Government, due to the nature of the co-operative enterprises which have been launched with Government support financially. Three members of the cabinet are men who have been identified closely with the Grain Growers' Movement. Hon. W. R. Motherwell has held portfolio as Minister of Agriculture for many years. Hon. George Langley, Minister of Municipal Affairs, helped to organize the farmers of Northern Saskatchewan in the early days. Finally in 1916 C. A. Dunning[1] resigned as general manager of the Saskatchewan Co-Operative Elevator Company to become the youngest Provincial Treasurer in Canada; for already the Saskatchewan Government had called upon him for service on two official commissions to investigate agriculture and finance in most of the European countries and his services were valuable.

Langley has been a prominent figure in Saskatchewan affairs ever since his arrival in the country in 1903. He was forty-one years old when he came and he brought with him long training as a public speaker, a knowledge of human nature and a ready twinkle in his eye for everything humorous. According to himself, his first job was chasing sparrows from the crops. After leaving the English rural life in which he was reared, he had worked on the London docks and as a London business man. In politics he became a disciple of the Cobden-Bright school and was one of the first members of the Fabian Society under the leadership of the redoubtable Bernard Shaw. It was Langley's habit, it is said, to talk to London crowds on side thoroughfares, standing on a soap-box and ringing a hand-bell to attract attention.

In becoming a Western Canadian farmer it did not take him long to slip around behind the problems of the farming class; for there was no greater adept at poking a cantankerous problem about with a sharp stick than the Honorable George. It was natural for this short, stout, bearded Englishman to gravitate into the first Legislature of the newly-formed Province of Saskatchewan and just as naturally he moved up to a place in the cabinet.

As one of the sponsors of the co-operative elevator scheme, by virtue of his place on the commission which recommended it, Langley has taken much interest in the co-operative activities of the farmers and on many occasions has acted as their spokesman.

With the relationships outlined it was to be expected that now and then opponents would hint that the Saskatchewan authorities had played politics with the farmers. Such charges, of course, are refuted indignantly. Knowing the widespread desire among the farmers themselves to keep free from political alliances, it would be a foolish government indeed which would fail to recognize that not to play politics was the best kind of politics that could be played.

Other leaders of sterling worth have contributed to the acknowledged success of co-operation in Saskatchewan, not forgetting John A. Maharg who came from Western Ontario in 1890 to settle near Moose Jaw. From the very beginning J. A. Maharg has worked for the cause of the farmers. A pioneer himself, he has a deep understanding of the Western Canadian farmers' problems and his devotion to their solution has earned him universal appreciation among the Grain Growers of Saskatchewan. Year after year he has been elected to the highest office in the gift of the Association. He has been President many times of both the Saskatchewan Grain Growers' Association and the Saskatchewan Co-Operative Elevator Company.

The Grain Growers' Movement, then, in this Province of Saskatchewan where it had its beginning, has grown to wonderful proportions with the passing of the years. Co-operation has been a pronounced success. The old conditions have passed far back down the trail. The new order of things has been fought for by men who have known the taste of smoky tea, the sour sweat of toil upon the land, the smell of the smudge fires on a still evening and the drive of the wind on the open plain. Out of the pioneer past they have stepped forward to the larger opportunities of the times—times which call for clear heads and wise vision.

For as they build for the future so will the Sons of the Movement watch and learn.

[1] The Union Government at Ottawa decided in February, 1918, to replace the office of Food Controller by the Canada Food Board, organized as a branch of the Dominion Department of Agriculture under Hon. T. A. Crerar. Hon. Charles A. Dunning was selected as Director of Production. The other members of the Canada Food Board were: H. B. Thomson, Chairman and Director of Conservation; J. D. McGregor, Director of Agricultural Labor. (Mr. McGregor resigned after a year in office.)

CHAPTER XX

WHAT HAPPENED IN ALBERTA

Beyond the fields we plough are others waiting,
The fallows of the ages all unknown.
Beyond the little harvests we are reaping
Are wider, grander harvests to be grown.

—Gerald J. Lively.

Out in the great Range Country all this time the United
Farmers were lickety-loping along the trail of difficulties that
carried their own special brand. The round-up revealed
increasing opportunities for service and one by one their
problems were cut out from the general herd, roped, tied and
duly attended to for the improvement of conditions in
Alberta. Here and there a difficulty persisted in breaking
away and running about bawling; but even these finally were
coralled.

Along with the Grain Growers of Manitoba and Saskatchewan
the United Farmers of Alberta had campaigned consistently
for government ownership of elevators, both provincial and
terminal. They had received assurance from Premier
Rutherford that if a satisfactory scheme could be evolved, the
Provincial Government was prepared to carry out the

establishment of a line of internal elevators in Alberta. It looked as if all that remained to be done was to follow the lead of Manitoba or Saskatchewan.

But on careful consideration neither of the plans followed in the other two provinces appeared to fit the special needs of the Alberta farmers. The province at the western end of the grain fields accordingly experienced quite a delay in obtaining elevator action.

In the meantime the discussion of terminal storage facilities was going on at Ottawa. The need for such facilities at Calgary and Vancouver was pressed by the Alberta representatives on various farmer delegations and finally the Dominion Government declared its intention of establishing internal elevators with full modern equipment at Moose Jaw and Saskatoon in Saskatchewan and at Calgary in Alberta; a Dominion Government terminal elevator at the Pacific Coast likewise was on the programme.

By this time the government operation of the Manitoba elevators had proved a complete failure and they had been leased by the Grain Growers' Grain Company. In Saskatchewan, however, the co-operative elevators were proving successful.

A close study of the co-operative scheme adopted in the province just east of them enabled the United Farmers of Alberta to work out a plan along similar lines. This was presented to the Premier, whose name meanwhile had changed from Rutherford to Sifton. The Act incorporating the Alberta Farmers' Co-Operative Elevator Company, Limited, was drafted in the spring of 1913 and passed unanimously by the Legislature. The new company held its first meeting in August, elected its officers[1] and went to work enthusiastically.

It had been decided by the United Farmers that full control and responsibility must rest in their own hands. They proposed to provide the means for raising at each point where an elevator was built sufficient funds to finance the purchase of grain at that point from their own resources, at the same time providing for the handling of other business than grain.

Under the Act the Provincial Government made cash advance of eighty-five per cent. of the cost of each elevator built or bought by the Company, but had no say whatever as to whether any particular elevator should be bought or built at any particular place, what it should cost or what its capacity or equipment should be. In security for the loan the Government took a first mortgage on the elevator and other property of the Company at the given point. The loans on elevators were repayable in twenty equal annual instalments.

The Company started off with the organization of forty-six Locals instead of the twenty which the Act called for and the construction of forty-two elevators was rushed. Ten additional elevators were bought. Although construction was not completed in time to catch the full season's business the number of bushels handled was 3,775,000, the Grain Growers' Grain Company acting as selling agent. By the end of the second year twenty-six more elevators had been built and the volume of grain handled had expanded to 5,040,000 bushels.

Now, this progress had been achieved in the face of continuous difficulties of one kind and another. Chief of these was the attempt to finance such a large amount of grain upon a small paid-up capital. The Company found that after finishing construction of the elevators they had no money with which to buy grain nor any assets available for bank borrowings. It was impossible to obtain credit upon the unpaid capital stock. The Provincial Government was approached for a guarantee of the account along the lines followed in Saskatchewan; but the Government refused to assume the responsibility.

It was at this juncture that the enemies of co-operation were afforded a practical demonstration of the fact that they had to deal not with any one farmers' organization but with them all. For the Grain Growers' Grain Company stepped into the breach with its powerful financial assistance.

The Alberta farmers were clamoring for the handling of farm supplies as well as grain; so that the young trading company in Alberta had its hands more than full to organize a full stride in usefulness from the start. The organization of the United Farmers of Alberta was growing very rapidly and the co-operative spirit was tremendously strong throughout the province. There was a demand for the handling of livestock shipments and soon it was necessary to establish a special Livestock Department.

It will be recalled that one of the subjects in which the Alberta farmers were interested from the first was the possibility of persuading the Provincial Government to undertake a co-operative pork-packing plant. Following the report of the Pork Commission upon the matter, however, official action on the part of the authorities had languished. The various committees appointed from year to year by the United Farmers gradually had acquired much valuable data and at last were forced to the conclusion that the development of a packing industry along co-operative lines was not so simple as it had appeared at first. Even in much older settled countries than Alberta the question, they found, had its complications. The first thing to discover was whether the farmers of a community were able and willing to adjust themselves to the requirements of an association for shipping stock together in carload lots to be sold at the large markets. Until such demonstration had been made it seemed advisable to defer the organization of a co-operative packing business.

After the formation of the Co-Operative Elevator Company, therefore, the Alberta farmers proceeded to encourage the co-operative shipment of livestock on consignment by their local unions. The Livestock Department entered the field first as buyers of hogs, handling 16,000 hogs in the first four months. The experiment bettered prices by half-a-cent per pound and the expansion of the Department began in earnest the following season when nearly 800 cars of hogs, cattle and sheep were handled.

On top of all the other troubles of the first year the farmers lost a valuable leader in the death of the president of the Co-Operative Elevator Company, W. J. Tregillus. Complete re-organization of the Executive was made and the question of his successor was considered from every angle. It was vital that no mistake be made in this connection and two of the directors were sent to study the business methods and policies of the Grain Growers' Grain Company and the Saskatchewan Co-Operative Elevator Company and to secure a General Manager. They failed to get in touch with anyone to fill the requirements and the management of both the other farmers' concerns expressed grave doubts as to the wisdom of a farmers' company looking for a manager whose training had been received with line elevator companies and who had not seen things from the farmer's side.

One of the remarkable features of the advance of the Farmers' Movement has been the manner in which strong leaders have stepped from their own ranks to meet every need. It has been a policy of the organized farmers to encourage the younger men to apply themselves actively in

Hopkins Moorhouse

the work in order that they might be qualified to take up the responsibilities of office when called upon. There are many outstanding examples of the wisdom of this in the various farmers' executives to-day; so that with the on-coming of the years there is little danger that sane, level-headed management will pass. Several of the men occupying prominent places to-day in the Farmers' Movement have grown up entirely under its tutelage.

So it turned out that in Alberta the man the farmers were seeking was one of themselves—one of the two directors sent out to locate a manager, in fact. His name was C. Rice-Jones. His father was an English Church clergyman whose work lay in the slum districts of London. This may have had something to do with the interest which the young man had in social problems. When at the age of sixteen he became a Canadian and went to work on various farms, finally homesteading in Alberta, that interest he carried with him. Out of his own experiences he began to apply it in practical ways and the Farmers' Movement drew him as a magnet draws steel. He became identified with the Veteran district eventually and there organized a local union. It was not long before he was in evidence in the wider field of the United Farmers' activities.

Fortunately the new President and General Manager of the Alberta Farmers' Co-Operative Elevator Company was not a man to lose his sense of direction in a muddle of affairs. Into the situation which awaited him he waded with consummate tact, discernment and push; so that it was not long before his associates were pulling with him for the fullest weight of intelligent effort. The difficulties were sorted and sifted and classified, the machinery oiled and running true, and with a valuable directorate at his back Rice-Jones "made good."

The third season of the Alberta Farmers' Co-operative

Elevator Company brought the final proof that the farmers knew how to support their own institutions. For through the 87 elevators that the farmers operated in Alberta flowed a total of nearly twenty million bushels of grain, with well over ten and one-quarter million bushels handled on commission. The Livestock Department in the face of severe competition achieved a permanent place in the livestock business of the province with offices of its own in the stock yards at Calgary and Edmonton. By this time livestock shipments had amounted to a value in excess of two million dollars. The Co-Operative Department had handled farm supplies to a total turnover of approximately $750,000.

As in the case of the Grain Growers' Grain Company and the Saskatchewan Grain Growers' Association's trading department the list of articles purchased co-operatively by the Alberta farmers grew very rapidly to include flour, feed, binder twine, coal, lumber and fence posts, wire fencing, fruit and vegetables, hay, salt, etc. In 1915-16 a thousand cars of these goods were purchased and distributed co-operatively, besides which a considerable volume of business was done in less-than-carload lots. Coal sheds were built in connection with many elevators, the staff increased and the entire Co-Operative Department thoroughly organized for prompt and satisfactory service.

[1] See Appendix—Par. 13.

CHAPTER XXI

IN THE DRAG OF THE HARROWS

"I see the villain in your face!"
"May it plaze yer worship, that must be a
personal reflection, sure."

—*Irish Wit and Humor (Howe).*

The "good old days" when the Farmer was a poor sheep without a shepherd, shorn to the pink hide with one tuft of wool left over his eyes—those "good old days" are gone forever. It is some time now since he became convinced that if a lion and a lamb ever did lie down together the lamb would not get a wink of sleep. As a matter of survival he has been making use of the interval to become a lion himself and the process has been productive of a great roaring in the Jungle.

All this co-operative purchasing of commodities in the three Prairie Provinces has not been developed to its present great volume without arousing antagonism in the business world. The co-operative idea in merchandizing is not confined to the West by any means. From the Atlantic to the Pacific various organizations have been formed to carry on business along co-operative lines. A Co-Operative Union has been formed to propagate the movement and the subject is vast.

But the establishment of an extending network of elevators under the control of the Western farmers has brought about possibilities which threaten to revolutionize the whole established commercial system. Farmers' Elevators in Dakota, Minnesota and Alberta have proved that it is practical to utilize the same staff at each point to manage the distribution of farm supplies as well as looking after elevator operation during the grain season. This being so, it is not difficult to visualize a great distributing system under centralized management with tremendous purchasing power.

There are those whose imaginations stretch readily to the extreme view that the Grain Growers are a menace. Such are filled with foreboding. They see the country merchant out of business and the whole business fabric destroyed.

"The farmers are talking everlastingly about 'a square deal,'" it is argued. "Why don't they practice what they preach and give the country merchant a square deal? What about the times of poor crops and money scarcity? Where would the farmer have been if the country merchant had not carried him on the books for the necessities of life?"

"It didn't cost the merchant anything to carry me," denies the farmer. "He just raised his prices to me and got credit from the wholesaler."

"Then what about the wholesaler?"

"Raised his prices and got credit from the manufacturer and the bank."

"Then the banks—"

"Refused to give me the credit in the first place!" interrupts the farmer resentfully. "Do you dare to blame me, Mister, for cutting out all these unnecessary middle charges when by proper organization I am able to finance myself and take advantage of cash discounts on the cost of living?"

That is the Farmer's motive for taking action. He wants to improve his scale of living for the sake of his family. By making the farm home a place of comfort his sons and daughters will be more content to remain on the land. He does not seek to hoard money; he intends to spend it. If middlemen are crowded out of his community it will be because there are too many of them. Instead of having to support parasites the community will be just that much more prosperous, the farms just that much better equipped, the land just that much more productive and thereby the country's wealth just that much greater.

That is how it appears to the Farmer.

"If the Farmer is to be a merchant, a wholesaler, a banker and all the rest of it he is no longer a farmer. Is nobody else to have a right to live?" enquires the Cynic. "Did these Grain Growers fight the elevator combine of the early days in order that they could establish a Farmers' Combine? Is one any better than the other?"

The inference is that the Grain Growers are bluffing deliberately and aiming at all the abuses conjured by the word, "combine." The slander is self-evident to anyone who examines the constitution of the Farmers' Movement, so framed from the first that any possibility of clique control was removed for all time. It is impossible to have a "combine" of fifty thousand units and maintain the necessary appeal to the cupidity of the individual. It is not possible for designing leaders, if such there were, to take even the first step in manipulation without discovery. It simply cannot be done. Woe betide the man who even exhibited such tendencies among his fellow Grain Growers! These organized farmers have learned how to do their own thinking and every rugged ounce of them is assertive. They are not to be fooled easily nor stampeded from their objective. And what is that objective?

"To play politics!" explodes the hidebound Party Politician knowingly.

"To get a share in the Divvy and eventually hog it!" suggests the Financial Adventurer.

"Equal opportunities to all; special privileges to none," the Grain Grower patiently reiterates.

He believes in doing away with "the Divvy" altogether. He believes that "the spoils system" is bad government and that no stone should be left unturned to elevate the living conditions of the Average Citizen to the highest possible plane. He believes that the status of a nation depends upon the status of its Average Citizen and in that he does not consider himself to be preaching Socialism but Common Sense.

Come back to the country store—to the Country Retailer who is pulling on the other end of the whiffle-tree with the Farmer for community progress. Each is necessary to the other and it is a vital matter if the co-operation of the Farmer is going to kill off a teammate, especially when tandeming right behind them are the Clydesdales of Commerce, the Wholesaler and the Manufacturer. With the Farmer kicking over the traces, the Retailer biting and squealing at the Wholesaler every little while and the Manufacturer with his ears laid back flat this distribution of merchandize in

Western Canada is no easy problem. It is bringing the Bankers to their aristocratic portals all along the route and about the only onlooker who is calm and serene is the Mail-Order Man as he passes overhead post-haste in the Government flying machine.

"I'd get along alright if the Farmer would pay up his debts to me," cries the Retailer. "I've been giving him too long a line of credit and now he's running rings around me and tying me up in a knot. When he gets some money he goes and buys from my competitors for cash or he buys more land and machinery. If I shorten the rope he busts it and runs away!"

"I'd be alright if everybody else would mind their own business," grumbles the Wholesaler. "Just trot along there now! Pay your bills, Farmer. Improve your service, Retailer. Don't ask me about high or low tariff. I've got my hands full with established lines and it's my business to supply them as cheaply as is consistent with quality. I want to see everybody succeed and it isn't fair to include me in any mix-up. Only the humming of that confounded flying-machine up there— Can't somebody bring down that Mail-Order bird? He isn't paying his share of the taxes while I've helped to finance this country."

"We shall come rejoicing, bringing in the sheaves," sings the Manufacturer. "Giddap, Dobbin!"

"'Money makes the mare go,'" quotes the Finance Minister, taking another look out of the window at the War Cloud. "'Money comes from the Soil,'" and he push-buttons a buzz-bell over in the Department of Agriculture.

"Send out the choir and let's have that 'Patriotism and Production' song again," is the order issued by some deputy sub-chief's assistant in response to the P. M.'s signal. "We must encourage our farmers to even nobler efforts."

And all the while the Unearned Increment loafs around, studying the Interest Charges which are ticking away like a taxicab meter, and the "Common Pee-pul" gaze in frozen fascination at the High Cost of Living flying its kite and climbing the string!

Seriously, though, the situation demands the earnest thought of all classes. The argument has so many facets that it is impossible within the limits of a few pages to present an adequate conception of all the vital problems that surround the Farmers' Movement. Each interest has its own data—packages of it—and it is difficult to know what to select and what to leave out and at the same time remain entirely fair to all concerned. There is some truth in many of the accusations which are bandied about. No new country can do without credit facilities. What about the homesteader or the poorer farmer who is starting on meagre resources? They will win through if given a chance. Who is to give it to them if business is put on a cash basis? On the other hand, is the man who has the cash to receive no consideration?

The trouble with our banks is that their system falls down when the retailer or the farmer need them most—in times of stringency. It is true that the wholesaler has done much for the country, that the retailer is often at the mercy of careless or selfish customers who abuse credit privileges. It is true that the mail-order houses also have performed good services in the general task of making a new country. The solution can be arrived at only by co-operation in its true sense—getting together—everybody. Also, while one may joke about "Patriotism and Production," the fact remains that much has been accomplished by these campaigns.

Asked if the organization of the farmers meant that the

retailer would be forced out of business, the well posted Credit Manager of a large Winnipeg wholesale establishment admitted that it would not mean that necessarily.

The same question put to C. Rice-Jones, President and Manager of the Alberta Farmers' Co-Operative Elevator Company, brought the same denial.

"The only men who would be weeded out," said he, "are those who have gone into the local store business without knowing anything about it and who can remain in it only because the present system allows them to charge any price they like. The men who know their business will remain. Those who are objecting to us are objecting to the very thing they have been doing themselves for fifty years—organizing."

"We want to farm, not to go into business," remarked H. W. Wood, President of the United Farmers of Alberta. "The local merchant gives us a local distribution service, a service which has to be given. We cannot destroy one single legitimate interest. But if there are four or five men living by giving a service that one man should give in a community and get just a living—that is what we are going to correct and we are absolutely entitled to do so. The selfishness we are accused of the accusers have practiced right along and these very things make it necessary for us to organize for self-protection. If they will co-operate with us to put their business on a legitimate basis we are willing to quit trying to do this business ourselves."

That is straight talk, surely. It is a challenge to the business men to meet the farmers half way for a better understanding. No problem ever was solved by extremists on either side. Enmity and suspicion must be submerged by sane discussion and mutual concessions bring about the beginnings of closer unity.

CHAPTER XXII

THE WIDTH OF THE FIELD

Our times are in His hand
Who saith, "A whole I planned,
Youth shows but half; trust
God; see all, nor be afraid."

—*Robert Browning.*

The Grain Growers' Movement in Western Canada now had attained potential proportions. In Saskatchewan, Manitoba and Alberta the Provincial Associations with their many Locals were in a flourishing condition. Each province was headquarters for a powerful farmers' trading organization to market grain and provide co-operative supplies. Unlike the Saskatchewan Co-Operative Elevator Company and the Alberta Farmers' Co-Operative Elevator Company, however, the pioneer business organization of the Grain Growers—the Grain Growers' Grain Company—was not provincial in scope but had a large number of shareholders in each of the three Prairie Provinces, in British Columbia and Ontario. Altogether, in 1916 the farmers owned and operated over 500 country elevators as well as terminal elevators to a capacity of three million bushels. The farmer shareholders in the three business concerns numbered more than 45,000.

During 1916 the farmers handled over ninety million bushels of their own grain.

With this remarkable growth the danger of rivalries and jealousies developing between their business organizations was a possibility upon which the farmers were keeping an eye. A certain amount of friendly competition was unavoidable. For some time, therefore, the necessity of closer union of their various organizations had been a serious topic among the leaders of the Grain Growers in all three provinces. It was the logical preparation for future achievements.

At its regular meetings in 1915 the Canadian Council of Agriculture—comprising officials representing the whole Grain Growers' Movement—had agreed that definite action would be desirable. A meeting of representatives from the respective Associations and companies interested accordingly was held in the offices of the Saskatchewan Co-Operative Elevator Company at Regina. The plan discussed was the formation of one large business concern, similar in a general way to the Wholesale Co-Operative Societies in the Old Country.

The idea was that this wholesale company should market and export grain, control terminal elevators and any manufacturing that might be done later on as well as importing supplies when necessary. This would leave each provincial company with its own organization to look after collection and distribution of supplies and to operate along the lines already existing in Saskatchewan and Alberta. The provincial companies would be in absolute control of the central or wholesale company.

A difference of opinion arose in regard to the method of selling grain. The representatives from the United Farmers of

Alberta, the Alberta Farmers' Co-Operative Elevator Company, the Manitoba Grain Growers' Association and the Grain Growers' Grain Company were unanimous in agreeing that it would be unwise to divide the marketing strength of the farmers into three parts instead of concentrating for fullest buying and selling power in the interest of the farmers in all three provinces. With the individual organizations each having a voice in the control of the central company there did not seem to them to be justification for carrying provincial divisions into the marketing machinery, thereby weakening it. With this view the Saskatchewan representatives could not agree, holding out for a separate selling channel for Saskatchewan grain.

A committee was appointed to try to work out some other solution to the problem of federating all three farmers' companies and a new proposal was submitted at a meeting of the Canadian Council of Agriculture, held in Winnipeg in July, 1916. This second attempt to get together was along the line of joint ownership of subsidiary concerns which would look after certain phases of the work—an export company, a terminal elevator company, the Public Press, Limited, and so on. However, the plan did not work out satisfactorily.

The feeling of the Alberta officials after the Regina meeting was that even if Saskatchewan were not ready at the present time to consider federation on a basis acceptable to the other provinces, this should not overthrow all idea of federation. In short, the Alberta directors were strongly of the opinion that, failing complete affiliation of the farmers' business organizations at this time, the organization in Alberta and the Grain Growers' Grain Company should get together nevertheless, and this suggestion they presented at the meeting of the Canadian Council of Agriculture in Winnipeg.

As this was approved by the Grain Growers' Grain Company

and the Manitoba Association officials steps were taken to go into the matter in detail, the Saskatchewan organization having signified its intention of withdrawing from present action. President C. Rice-Jones, of the Alberta Farmers' Co-Operative Elevator Company, and President T. A. Crerar, of the Grain Growers' Grain Company, were asked to give the matter careful thought and make their recommendations to their respective boards of directors.

There followed a joint meeting of all those interested. It was held at Winnipeg and the result was a recommendation that the Alberta Farmers' Co-Operative Elevator Company and the Grain Growers' Grain Company be amalgamated under the name "United Grain Growers, Limited." [1] When the matter finally came before the farmers concerned—at their annual meetings in 1916—it was decided unanimously to go ahead with the amalgamation of these two farmers' business organizations.

Accordingly application was made for necessary changes in the charter of the Grain Growers' Grain Company and these changes were granted by Act of the Dominion Parliament in June, 1917. The authorized capital stock of United Grain Growers is five million dollars. Its annual meetings are to be held in the different provinces alternately. The shareholders are formed into local groups, each represented by delegates at annual meetings, these delegates alone doing the voting. Proxy voting is not allowed. The charter is designed, in brief, to introduce the system of internal government that has been in practice by the Alberta Farmers' Co-Operative Elevator Company and the Saskatchewan Co-Operative Elevator Company and has proved so satisfactory in every way.

This "merger" is unique in that the objections to a monopoly cannot be urged against it. There is no watered stock. With proxy voting eliminated no group of men can gain control of the company's affairs. Stock holdings by individuals is limited to $2,000 on a capitalization of five million and no man can grow rich by speculation with assets. Instead of exploiting the public the aim is service—reduction of prices instead of inflation.

United Grain Growers, Limited, have begun their first year's business as an amalgamated farmers' concern, all the final details having been settled to the entire satisfaction of the farmers interested.

The fact that the Saskatchewan Grain Growers' executives did not decide to amalgamate their co-operative marketing machinery with that of the others just now must not be misconstrued as a lack of harmony among the leaders of these powerful institutions. For they are meeting constantly in their inter-provincial relations, for mutual business advantages and in the broader educational aspects of the entire Movement.

It will be seen that with such complete and solid business resources established in the three Prairie Provinces the organized farmers have been in a position to widen their field of influence and to carry on much propaganda work. The Movement has spread steadily until it embraces organization in other than prairie provinces. There seems to be a tendency among the entire agricultural population of Canada to organize and co-operate; so that it is not impossible for Canadian farmers in time to have a unity of organization in every province of the Dominion.

In Ontario for many years there have been various farmers clubs, associations or granges. Until 1914 these were merely disorganized units. At the annual meeting of the Dominion Grange, however—December 17th and 18th, 1913—the advisability of consolidating for greater co-operation was discussed at some length. Representatives from the Western Grain Growers were present and told the story of what the Western farmer had accomplished. A committee[2] was appointed and, after investigating rural conditions in Ontario, this committee called a convention for March 19th and 20th, 1914, at Toronto. Farmers and fruit growers turned out in strength, old-time organization was cast aside and there came into being the "United Farmers of Ontario," [2] and the "United Farmers' Co-Operative Company, Limited," [3] with aims and organization similar to those of the Grain Growers.

Although practically born during the war—although conditions have been far from normal, the United Farmers of Ontario have progressed steadily and naturally, with the co-operative activities setting the pace and with efficient service as the watchword. By 1915 there were 126 local associations with a total membership of 5,000. In the face of bad climatic conditions and war disturbances 1916 found the young organization being looked upon by the Ontario agriculturists with interest instead of suspicion. It continued to grow of its own accord. By that is meant that no advertising or other energetic campaign was undertaken; yet the membership increased during the year to 8,000 with 200 Locals organized throughout the province. To-day there is a total membership in excess of twenty thousand throughout the Province. Local conventions, addressed by Western leaders and other qualified speakers, have become a feature of the development.

The first month in business for the United Farmers' Co-Operative Company was September, 1914, when $827 was taken in. The next month the sales increased to $6,250, and in November to $8,214. The December sales jumped to $17,970. The sales for 1915 approximated $226,000. In 1916 this amount was nearly doubled and during the first five months of 1917 the business done reached a total of $513,000. All this on paid-up capital of only $5,000. The

Ontario Company has secured a new charter, increasing its authorized capital from $10,000 to $250,000.

This expansion has been very satisfactory in view of the special conditions which necessarily make the progress of the Movement in the East slower than in the West. Ontario crops varying widely in different districts, the same unity of interest which has made possible the large grain companies of the West does not obtain. The Ontario farmers have had to confine their efforts to commercial lines. Co-operative sale of livestock, cheese, etc., may develop in time. Also the farm population in Ontario is in the minority and there are few electoral divisions where the urban vote does not control, resulting in mixed issues unknown on the prairies. Powerful influences have been brought to bear to handicap the Farmers' Movement in Ontario; but nevertheless it is spreading so rapidly that with the proper educational campaign great possibilities lie ahead of the Ontario farmers.

The United Farmers of Ontario now have become affiliated with the Canadian Council of Agriculture,[4] the inter-provincial body of the organized farmers of Canada. The farmers of Nova Scotia, Prince Edward Island and Quebec are showing much interest and have sought to have the Movement extended. Meetings have been held and no doubt in due course the Eastern farmers will be prepared for unity of action in every province.

What about British Columbia? On February 16th, 1917, the "United Farmers of British Columbia" was a development in the Pacific Coast Province. Prior to this there had been quite a number of individual farmers' organizations scattered through-out the agricultural sections of British Columbia. The initiative for closer unity was taken by the Cowichan Creamery Association, which called a meeting of the farmers in the Cowichan district to discuss the cost of production and serious labor conditions which were threatening complete failure of agriculture in British Columbia. At this meeting what was called temporarily the "Vancouver Island Farmers' Union" was formed with over one hundred members. Representatives from other districts were on hand to assure the expansion of the movement and a provisional organization committee[5] was appointed to carry on the missionary work.

This Provisional Committee—called into existence by a mass meeting of farmers held at Duncan, B.C., on November 4th, 1916—at once prepared a strong circular, setting forth the case of the farmers and the need for organization. This was sent out to the secretaries of all Farmers' Institutes and suggested that a special meeting of delegates should be held at Victoria when the usual farmers' conventions were in session a few months later. Thus came about the final large organization meeting of February 16th, 1917, which resulted in the "United Farmers of British Columbia," with strong membership under the guidance of enthusiastic officers.[6]

Representatives of the Grain Growers, from Alberta and Manitoba, were present to lend the encouragement of their experience. Among them was Roderick McKenzie, then Secretary[7] of the Canadian Council of Agriculture. When the farmers commenced organization in Manitoba, he said, it was possible to find many old-fashioned farmers who could see no reason for organization. Had not their fathers been successful farmers? Had they not raised a family of eight or ten or a dozen or more without belonging to any organization?—educated them, too? These old-time farmers forgot that the world was making progress as the years went by and they were not living in the same age as their fathers before them.

"Fifty years ago, when I was a boy," Mr. McKenzie continued, "there was no such thing as a joint stock company. We would not hear a word about combines or trusts or transportation organizations or financial institutions. At that time the business was carried on by individuals. Then it grew into partnerships. From partnerships it developed into joint stock corporations and now we have these forming into trusts and combines and holding companies. It is simply co-operation of the few in the interests of the few. It created a force in public affairs and this must be met by another force—the organization of the common people, led by the farmers.

"Where would the British Army be as a disorganized army confronting the Germans? Nowhere! Place a body of disorganized farmers in front of organized industrial interests and you see where you are at! There is no form of industry, no form of labor, no form of finance, banking associations, loan associations, insurance compensation associations, transportation associations, that are not organized. In Winnipeg we have a Bootblack's Association and each of the little fellows contributes five dollars a year to the support of their organization and five dollars represents fifty pairs of boots to blacken at a dime the pair.

"In our Grain Growers' associations the organization is simple and coherent. There is no pass-word. There is no grip. There is no riding of the goat. We don't ask a farmer whether he is a Grit or a Tory; we don't ask him anything about his nationality or his relations or where he comes from or anything else. One of the main aims of the organization is to make good Canadians of the different nationalities we have in this Western country. We are getting the Galicians and other nationalities gradually brought in—getting them together for the development of Canadianism and the community spirit.

"The one thing we have steered clear of is letting party politics enter into our organization. The thing we are trying to do is to co-operate with our legislators by helping them to find out the things that need enacting into law and that have not been enacted into law or to find what laws already on the statute books are weak and ask that these weaknesses be corrected—not in a dominating spirit but in a spirit of equity."

Public opinion is rallying to the leadership of the farmers. Their policy is progressive. Probably the first body in Canada to give Woman her proper place in its activities and councils was the Saskatchewan Grain Growers' Association. To-day the farm women of the West are organized with the Grain Growers in all three Prairie Provinces, working side by side. Their aims are to solve the many problems directly bearing upon home life, educational facilities, health and all things which affect the farm woman's life and they have been of great assistance in many ways, particularly in Red Cross and other patriotic endeavors. To do justice to the noble efforts of Western Canada's farm women would require a separate volume.

Still another development with far-reaching possibilities is the tendency of the Grain Growers and the Church to get together. It first revealed itself in Alberta under the conscientious encouragement of President H. W. Wood, of the United Farmers of Alberta, when in 1916 he inaugurated "U.F.A. Sunday"—one Sunday in each year to be set aside as the Farmers' own particular day, with special sermons and services. It was born of a realization that something is fundamentally wrong with our social institutions and that "the Church will have to take broader responsibilities than it is now doing."

"Is Christ to develop the individuals and Carl Marx mobilize and lead them?" asked Mr. Wood. "Is Christ to hew the stones and Henry George build them into the finished edifice? If Christ cannot mobilize His forces and build true civilization His name will be forgotten in the earth. The solution of the economic problems must be spiritual rather than intellectual. This is the work of the Church and the Church must take the responsibility for it."

Not only did the idea of a special Sunday meet with hearty response from the churches and farmers in Alberta, but it was taken up in Manitoba and Saskatchewan. In 1917 "Grain Growers' Sunday" was observed all over the West and led to many inspiring addresses. One of the most significant of these was delivered by President J. A. Maharg, of the Saskatchewan Grain Growers' Association, at a mass meeting in Moose Jaw on Sunday, May 27th.

"There has been a strong agitation against church union," said Mr. Maharg. "We hope to bring the churches together. The establishment of community churches is not altogether an impossibility. That groups of churches will be brought together for the holding of community services is not altogether impossible, and a farmers' organization is not an organization that is farthest away from doing this."

In these days of revolutionary thought who shall set the length and width of the Farmers' field of influence, therefore? A string of co-related provincial organizations of farmers, stretching right across the Dominion, working harmoniously through the Canadian Council of Agriculture, will create a national force which in itself will represent Public Opinion—which cannot be denied the upward trend to wider and better citizenship for all classes in Canada.

For Public Opinion governs legislation as legislation governs the country.

[1] See Appendix—Par. 17.

[2] See Appendix—Par. 14.

[3] See Appendix—Par. 15.

[4] See Appendix—Par. 11.

[5] See Appendix—Par. 16.

[6] See Appendix—Par. 16.

[7] See Appendix—Par. 18.

CHAPTER XXIII

THE DEPTH OF THE FURROWS

Men at some time are masters of their fates:
The fault, dear Brutus, is not in our stars,
But in ourselves, that we are underlings.

—Julius Caesar.

Because it was the logical and primary source of redress for the abuses which led the Western farmers to organize, the Grain Growers from the first have concerned themselves seriously with legislation. It took them a little while to discover that instead of being an all-sufficient panacea, mere legislation may become at times as flat and useless as a cold pancake. But by the time the farmers had come to close quarters with their difficulties their vision had widened so that they were able to look ahead, clearing the path for the next step forward. So frequently have they besought the Governments, both Federal and Provincial, that occasionally they have been accused by harassed politicians of "playing politics and nothing else."

As their organizations grew and acquired knowledge it is true that these "petitioners" who "did humbly pray" began to straighten their backs a little, the while they wrestled with the kinks that were bothering them from too much stooping. It was a sort of chiropractic process for the alleviation of growing pains—the discovery of the proper nerve to ask and receive, to seek and find. As the People grew more accustomed to the sound of their own Voice it was only natural that the quaver of timidity began to disappear from the tones of it and that their speech grew stronger in the Legislative Halls dedicated to government "of, by and for" them. The "Backbone of His Country" set out to prove that he was not spineless, merely disjointed. And as he gained confidence in his vertebrae the Farmer began to sit up and take notice—began even to entertain the bold idea of getting eventually upon his feet.

The intention was laudable. To make it audible he assembled a platform, stood up on it, and argued. His protests could be heard clean to the back of the Hall. Like the young elephant whose trunk was being stretched by the crocodile, he said: "You are hurting me!" In the nose-pulling game of Party Politics as it too often has been played, it sometimes takes a lusty holler to make itself heard above all the other hollering that is going on; if getting a hearing is "playing politics," then the Grain Growers have run up a pretty good score.

They began with various amendments to the Grain Act. These included the famous "car distribution" clause, the farmer's right to a car and his procedure to obtain it and additional cars as he needed them, the provision of penalties for the purchase or sale of car rights, etc. Opposition to some of these amendments was keen and the farmers had to fight constantly; when they were not fighting for necessary amendments they were fighting to retain those already secured. Constant vigilance was required. Many delegations of Grain Growers visited Ottawa from time to time to plead for improvement of conditions in handling grain, more equitable inspection methods, government ownership and operation of terminal facilities and so on.

Each year the annual conventions of the various associations in Saskatchewan, Manitoba and Alberta grew in size and importance; each year the Grain Growers' knowledge expanded, much of it gained by marketing experience. From these "Farmers' Parliaments" and the pages of the *Grain Growers' Guide* they drew inspiration for many radical ideas and threshed them out into well defined policies. By the time Sir Wilfrid Laurier, then Premier of Canada, ventured West in 1910 the farmers were pretty well posted on national topics. Everywhere he went he faced thousands of ruddy, big-fisted men who read addresses to him and did a lot of extemporaneous talking which was no less forceful and complete than the prepared briefs.

Six or eight hundred of them followed him back to Ottawa in December of that same year and laid siege to the Government on its own stamping-ground. It was the most remarkable red-seal record of the Voice from the Soil that hitherto had been known thereabouts. In order that there might be no doubt as to the planks on which they stood, the Grain Growers assembled a platform in full view of the audience.

"We want reciprocal Free Trade between Canada and the United States in all horticultural, agricultural and animal products," declared the farmers; "also in spraying materials and fertilizers; illuminating, fuel and lubricating oils; cement, fish and lumber.

"We want reciprocal Free Trade between the two countries in all agricultural implements, machinery, vehicles and parts of each of these. We want it carried into effect through the independent action of the respective Governments rather than by the hard and fast requirements of a treaty.

"We want the duties on all British goods lowered to one-half the rates charged under the general tariff schedule, whatever that may be. Also, we want any trade advantages given to the United States in reciprocal trade relations to be extended to Great Britain.

"We want such further gradual reduction of the remaining preferential tariff as will ensure the establishment of complete free trade between Canada and the Mother Land within ten years. We're willing to face direct taxation, in such form as may be advisable, to make up the revenue required under new tariff conditions."

"This bunch wants the whole earth!" cried the Canadian Manufacturers indignantly.

"Sub-soil and all!" nodded the Railways.

"Certainly they're plowing deep," commented the Banks.

"To eradicate weeds," admitted the Farmers.

"Damn it all, anyway!" worried the Politicians.

To show that they were talking neither Tory nor Grit, the Western farmers proceeded to waylay the Leader of the Opposition, Hon. R. L. Borden, the following year when he in turn decided to "Go West." He, too, came face to face with thousands of ruddy, big-fisted men and listened to their equally plain-spoken addresses, prepared and extemporaneous.

And what came of it all? Did these farmers get what they wanted?

Not yet!

But while all this agitation of the Grain Growers one time and another seldom has resulted in assent to their full requests, certain compliances have been made on different occasions with beneficial results. For instance—to mention three—the Royal Grain Commission of 1906, the permanent Grain Commission, and the Government Terminal Elevators are an outcome of various requests and delegations of the Grain Growers.

Certainly the organized farmers of Western Canada have attained a measure of self-confidence which enables them to declare themselves in definite language. While seeking wider markets and the real value of their products, they have been opposed always to any scheme which accomplishes higher prices at the expense of the consumer or of the British workman. They do not believe in import duties on food stuffs, clothing, fuel or building material. Rather do they favor bringing closer together the producer and consumer to the advantage of both. They believe in cheaper money for the development of agriculture and other industries and in such utilization of natural resources that the homes of the people may be improved.

They have stood consistently behind woman suffrage and the abolition of the liquor traffic. They would adopt direct legislation through the Initiative and Referendum. They believe in the principles of Co-Operation in buying and selling. They have urged extension of the parcel post system, the reduction of traffic charges to a reasonable basis, Government control of waterways and all natural resources that they may be developed only in the public interest.

Does a creed like this spell class legislation? Does it indicate that in his eagerness to improve the conditions surrounding his own life the Grain Grower is forgetting the general welfare of the Dominion of Canada? Listen to the doctrine which the leaders have inculcated on every occasion—to President T. A. Crerar before the War:

"You have a very clear-cut and distinct responsibility in supporting the whole movement of the organized farmers in Western Canada; for this means that you are improving not alone your own environment and condition, but also creating the conditions and influences that will develop a higher and purer ideal of public service upon the part of our people than we have in Canada to-day. It should be a source of great satisfaction that upon all important matters the policies adopted and supported by the organized farmers in the past have been formed upon what in their judgment would benefit the country as a whole and not from the narrow view of selfish interest.

"During the past ten years the people of Canada have mortgaged the prosperity of the future to far too great an extent. Our total borrowings as a nation, for public and private purposes, have run into such a colossal sum that it requires about $160,000,000 annually to pay interest on the amounts borrowed. This constitutes a very heavy task on a country with about eight millions of a population. Manufacturing industries have been built up with a view of developing home industry and furnishing home markets, but often at a very heavy cost to our agricultural development, with the result that we have been travelling in a circle, reaching nowhere, rather than along the road that leads to Progress.

"We hear considerable nowadays of the necessity of a 'Back to the Land' movement. It is necessary, however, to do a little more than get people located on the land with a view of increasing agricultural production. It is necessary to free agriculture from the burdens now resting upon it and make it the first business of the country.

"Much of our natural resources has been recklessly handled, and as a people we are faced with the necessity of overcoming the evil effects of our unbusinesslike methods as a nation in administering resources. If we are to surmount our short-comings in this respect and pay our obligations as a nation to the outside world, we must place agriculture throughout Canada upon a thoroughly sound and profitable basis. The creation of wealth from our wonderfully rich natural resources, in which agriculture stands in the forefront, is the essential thing and should receive most consideration from our Governments—both Dominion and Provincial.

"We must learn to respect each other's differences and, if we do, with the development of that democratic spirit which is now day by day becoming more manifest in Western Canada, we need have no fear of our usefulness as an agency in bringing about the ultimate triumph of the principles of justice between man and man."

Listen to President J. A. Maharg, addressing the Saskatchewan Grain Growers' Association in 1914:

"What is wanted is the general recognition by all classes of the importance of Agriculture and an honest desire by them to assist in placing it on a basis equal to that of any other industry—making it an occupation that will draw people to it instead of driving them away. In soliciting the aid of other classes I am not asking them to assist us in gaining any special favors whatever; all we ask is that they assist us to have Agriculture placed in the position its importance entitles it to."

Hear the President of the United Farmers of Alberta, H. W. Wood:

"This is the day of class co-operation. That means inter-class competition. In this competition of class against class ours is the losing class at every turn because we have been the least organized, the least co-operative; consequently the weakest. Before we can hope to hold our own in this struggle we will have to bring our full strength, thoroughly organized, to bear in protection of our rights.

"I have an abiding faith that the organized farmers will receive that strength, not selfishly but unselfishly in the defence of the rights of all and for the spoliation of none. The highest ambition I have for our organization is that it may develop along the lines of safety and sanity, that we may hold to a steady determination to go forward unwaveringly in our efforts till the door of hope and opportunity is as wide open to the farmers as to any class in the world, that we may zealously cultivate unselfish co-operation and learn to treat fairly and justly every man and every class that is giving a useful service to society."

And this from the Presidential address of R. C. Henders at the last Manitoba Grain Growers' convention:

"In order to have legislation that will be equitable to the different interests concerned, all of these interests should be somewhat equally represented in the passing of such legislation. We do not desire to minimize in any way the great commercial interests of our people, yet we feel that the work of our associations is educational and legislative in its character. Democratic rule requires that the average citizen be an active, instructed and intelligent ruler of his country and therefore the success of democracy depends upon the education of the people along two principal lines—first, political knowledge; second, and what is of far more importance, political morality. Ideal government is found when we have righteous rulers governing a people of character and intelligence. Right education is right thinking and right thinking can only come through accurate information."

Now, is all this preaching of the men who are leading the farmers just so much talk?—chaff?—prairie wind?

If not, what lies back of it? The farmers have an organization which meets every so-often to harmonize and crystallize the thought among their various associations and business units. It is that same Canadian Council of Agriculture which has been mentioned already. It consists of the executive committees of eight farmers' co-operative, business and educational institutions, to wit: The United Farmers of Ontario, The United Farmers' Co-Operative Company of Ontario, The Grain Growers' Association of Manitoba, United Grain Growers (of the entire West), The Grain Growers' Association of Saskatchewan, The Saskatchewan Co-Operative Elevator Company, The United Farmers of Alberta, and the *Grain Growers' Guide*, the official organ of the whole movement.

At a meeting of this influential body in Winnipeg in December, 1916—representing an affiliation of 60,000 farmers—a "National Political Platform" was adopted to embrace economic, political and social reforms not alone in the interests of the farmers but of Canada's citizens generally. The farmers are looking for the support of all who live in cities and towns as well as the rural districts; of organized Labor as well as organized farmers.

This platform was referred to the provincial organizations which stand behind the Canadian Council of Agriculture. It was considered by each of the provincial boards and by them referred in turn to the three thousand local community associations into which the members are organized. Each Local was asked to call a meeting to consider the platform and vote upon its adoption. The next step was for the members to give their votes and financial support only to such candidates for the House of Commons as would pledge support of this National Platform in its entirety and who could be relied upon as Members of Parliament to live up to their pledges.

And here is the National Political Platform on which the farmers stand without equivocation:

THE CUSTOMS TARIFF

WHEREAS the war has revealed the amazing financial strength of Great Britain, which has enabled her to finance not only her own part in the struggle, but also to assist in financing her Allies to the extent of hundreds of millions of pounds, this enviable position being due to the free trade policy which has enabled her to draw her supplies freely from every quarter of the globe and consequently to undersell her competitors on the world's markets, and because this policy has not only been profitable to Great Britain but has greatly strengthened the bonds of Empire by facilitating trade between the Motherland and her overseas Dominions—we believe that the best interests of the Empire and of Canada would be served by reciprocal action on the part of Canada through gradual reductions of the tariff on British imports, having for its object a closer union and a better understanding between Canada and the Motherland, and by so doing not only strengthen the hands of Great Britain in the life and death struggle in which she is now engaged, but at the same time bring about a great reduction in the cost of living to our Canadian people;

AND WHEREAS the protective tariff has fostered combines,

trusts and "gentlemen's agreements" in almost every line of Canadian industrial enterprise, by means of which the people of Canada—both urban and rural—have been shamefully exploited through the elimination of competition, the ruination of many of our smaller industries and the advancement of prices on practically all manufactured goods to the full extent permitted by the tariff;

AND WHEREAS agriculture—the basic industry upon which the success of all other industries primarily depends—is almost stagnant throughout Canada as shown by the declining rural population in both Eastern and Western Canada, due largely to the greatly increased cost of agricultural implements and machinery, clothing, boots and shoes, building material and practically everything the farmer has to buy, caused by the protective tariff, so that it is becoming impossible for farmers generally to carry on farming operations profitably;

AND WHEREAS the protective tariff is the most wasteful and costly method ever designed for raising national revenue, because for every dollar obtained thereby for the public treasury at least three dollars pass into the pockets of the protected interests, thereby building up a privileged class at the expense of the masses, thus making the rich richer and the poor poorer;

AND WHEREAS the protective tariff has been and is a chief corrupting influence in our national life because the protected interests, in order to maintain their unjust privileges, have contributed lavishly to political and campaign funds, thus encouraging both political parties to look to them for support, thereby lowering the standard of public morality;

THEREFORE BE IT RESOLVED that the Canadian Council of Agriculture, representing the organized farmers of Canada, urges that as a means of bringing about these much needed reforms and at the same time reducing the high cost of living, now proving such a burden on the people of Canada, our tariff laws should be amended as follows:

(1) By reducing the customs duty on goods imported from Great Britain to one half the rates charged under the general tariff and that further gradual, uniform reductions be made in the remaining tariff on British imports that will ensure complete free trade between Great Britain and Canada in five years.

(2) That the Reciprocity Agreement of 1911, which still remains on the United States statute books, be accepted by the Parliament of Canada.

(3) That all food stuffs not included in the Reciprocity Agreement be placed on the free list.

(4) That agricultural implements, farm machinery, vehicles, fertilizer, coal, lumber, cement, illuminating fuel and lubricating oils be placed on the free list.

(5) That the customs tariff on all the necessaries of life be materially reduced.

(6) That all tariff concessions granted to other countries be immediately extended to Great Britain.

TAXATION FOR REVENUE

As these tariff reductions will very considerably reduce the national revenue derived from that source, the Canadian Council of Agriculture would recommend that in order to provide the necessary additional revenue for carrying on the government of the country and for the prosecution of the war to a successful conclusion, direct taxation be imposed in the following manner:

(1) By a direct tax on unimproved land values, including all natural resources.

(2) By a sharply graduated personal income tax.

(3) By a heavy graduated inheritance tax on large estates.

(4) By a graduated income tax on the profits of corporations.

OTHER NECESSARY REFORMS

The Canadian Council of Agriculture desires to endorse also the following policies as in the best interests of the people of Canada:

(1) The nationalization of all railway, telegraph and express companies.

(2) That no more natural resources be alienated from the Crown but brought into use only under short term leases, in which the interests of the public shall be properly safeguarded, such leases to be granted only by public auction.

(3) Direct legislation, including the initiative and referendum and the right of recall.

(4) Publicity of political campaign fund contributions and expenditures both before and after elections.

(5) The abolition of the patronage system.

(6) Full provincial autonomy in liquor legislation, including manufacture, export and import.

(7) That the extension of the franchise to women in any province shall automatically admit them to the federal franchise.

That is the official stand of the farmers and they point out that their political platform[1] is constructive, not destructive. The farmers are not trying to sidestep their fair share of the expenses in connection with government and public institutions; where they have torn down they have rebuilt.

Admitting that the prosperity of Western Canada is essential to our national prosperity, it is not necessary to look far in order to understand why the farmers have taken this definite action. Western farmers and citizens generally are carrying extra burdens which offset the advantages of cheap and fertile land. Interest on mortgages and bank loans have been higher than in Eastern Canada. It is more expensive to distribute commodities West than East. On account of the lavish donations of Western lands to railway promoters the cost of railway construction has borne heavily on the West. Freight rates are about sixty per cent. higher and express rates about sixty-six per cent. higher than in Eastern Canada. Thanks to the protective tariff, Western people are paying high for everything they get without any return compensation.

"Something has to be done to lift some of these unjust burdens," say the farmers, "if a prosperous country is to be developed West of the Great Lakes."

Hence this platform. The Western farmers believe in it earnestly. It is their politics. They believe that the results which would follow its support in the House of Commons would be of untold benefit to the Canadian people as a whole. They will continue to believe it.

When the crisis arose which brought about the last election, in which Union Government swept the West, the farmers saw the gravity of the situation and were prepared to forego immediate discussion of tariff amendments to concentrate on winning the war. Some of the farmers' candidates even withdrew in favor of Union candidates. All those who remained in the field were elected.

After the war is won—what? Reforms of breathtaking sweep are taking place as the natural outcome of current conditions. The liquor traffic has been tossed aside like a useless boot. Woman has stepped forth to a sphere of active worth without upheaval. Just where lie the boundaries of the impossible and who shall define them?

It is a far-seeing, clear-thinking New Farmer who has come forward in the last decade. Through his associations, his marketing experiences, his contact with railways and banks and manufacturers and governments he has become a student of economics. At the same time he has strengthened his thews and sinews for whatever may face him on the path ahead.

And his eyes are wide open to the fact that there are "lions in the path!"

Wait a minute, Mr. Business Man! Before condemning this Western farmer out of hand, put yourself in his place and try for a moment in all fairness to forget your own viewpoint. It may be that you have not even seen the prairies. Have you ever been at sea with not a thing in sight but water, sky, horizon? Imagine the water to be land, and yourself living in a one-room shack or a little low sod hut bewhiskered with growing grass. The nearest railway was fifty miles away and you got so lonesome that the howl of a coyote or the cry of owls in the night nearly drove you crazy. Neighbors so scarce your social pleasures were cut off by distance and you reared your family on that homestead twenty-five miles from a doctor, a church or a school.

When you made the long trip in for supplies in those early days you found you had to pay anywhere up to twice as much as their market value while for what you had to sell you had to take from twenty-five to fifty per cent. less than the market value. The implements you simply had to have for your work you bought on the instalment plan with interest at ten and twelve per cent. for the privilege.

When you had survived three years of this and with high hopes took your patent to the mortgage company to raise a loan at ten per cent. you found you couldn't get accommodation. Thereupon in marched your implement and other creditors with a chattel mortgage on everything you had—except the missus and the kids and the baby's bottley-by!

Then in the beautiful hot month of August it blew up black one day and the chickens scurried for shelter and you and the wife stood with your noses flattened against the window-pane—unless it was only oiled paper—and watched the big ice-marbles bouncing and heard the hail drumming flat in a few minutes the acres of wheat you had worked so hard to produce.

Or perhaps you escaped that time only to have your wheat frozen later on and when you took three days on purpose to haul in a wagonload to the elevator you couldn't get a decent offer for it. So that you pulled off your mitts and clenched your frost-cracked hands as you prepared to turn homeward with but a pitiful portion of the food and clothing you had promised the family you would bring. As you spread across your chest, inside your sheepskin coat, the old newspaper somebody had given you would your soul expand with the joy of living while you headed out into the snowy waste at forty degrees below zero?

And if after you got home and the crying young ones had been put to bed in the corner behind the canvas curtain and your wife came and sat beside you, her own tears bravely dried—if then you read in the paper that the Government had decided you farmers were so prosperous you should contribute from your easily gained wealth a free gift to manufacturers, financiers, railway magnates or others—then would you say with a great booming, hearty enthusiasm and shining eyes: "I tell you, Wife, this is the life!"—would you?

Or would you just proceed to swear—naturally, successfully, in what is known as "flowing" language?

By just such pioneer hardships were the farmers of Western Canada driven to organize in self-defence. It has ever been the history of revolt that its wellspring was the suffering of the people. Pioneer hardships it was that caused the various movements which agitated the farmers of the Western States in earlier days. When fingers become hardened and crooked from unceasing toil that achieves nothing but premature old age; when hope withers in a treadmill that grinds to the very soul—then comes rebellion.

[1] Since the formation of the organized farmers' National Political Platform several of its planks have been adopted as legislation at Ottawa, notably the abolition of the patronage system, extension of the franchise to women, total prohibition, and personal income taxation.

CHAPTER XXIV

AND THE END IS NOT YET

The principle of co-operation draws the whole community together. It breaks down barriers. It unites the State. It gives hope to the humblest toiler. And it strengthens the great moral ideal of duty, without which no State can endure.

—Earl Grey.

What is to be the final outcome of the Western farmers' revolt and its spread to rural communities in Eastern provinces? Is there to be greater harmony among opposing interests or is Canada on the threshold of internal strife which will plow deep furrows of dissension between class and class to an extent hitherto unknown in this country? If there is to be a pitched fight between capitalistic groups and the people at large, led by the farmers, what are the chances of victory for the latter? If they win, what will be the national effect?

These were a few of the questions which first turned the writer's serious attention to the Grain Growers. It seems scarcely credible that this great economic movement has attained present momentum practically unheralded; yet such is the case. The writer had watched its early struggles to success from Government windows and as preparation for a brief historical sketch it seemed desirable to get out among the farmers themselves and study the situation from their angle.

Frankly, the task was not approached without some skepticism as to the motives which might be uncovered. Almost the only occasions on which the Grain Growers revealed themselves to the public were when they waited upon politicians for this, that or the other. So often did this happen and so insistent were they that there seemed some grounds for the belief that to satisfy a Grain Grower was humanly impossible. From Legislative casements it even looked at times as if they were a new species of Indian, collecting political scalps! All manner of people accused them of all manner of things. In the East they were called "blacksmith-shop politicians, nail-keg economists, grousers and soreheads"; in the West they were dubbed "corner-grocer statesmen and political football players."

When the caravans of the Eastern political chieftains, Liberal and Conservative, came West they knew they were going to be held up by the outlaws. Long before these respective expeditions started across the plains infested with wild and dangerous Grain Growers, their scouts—the Western M.P.'s —were ranging far and wide in preparation.

And when those Grain Growers in turn rode East to take possession of Ottawa there was a popular expectation that they were about to whoop in and shoot up the town in the real old wild and woolly way. They were referred to cleverly as "Sod-Busters." It was rather startling to find them merely a new type of Business Farmer, trained to think on his feet, a student of economics.

To gather and verify the facts here recorded has required two years. During that time the writer has listened to earnest farmers in prairie shacks, pioneers and newcomers, leaders and followers, and has watched these farmers at work in their "Farmers' Parliaments" where they assemble annually by the thousands. It is impossible thus to meet and know these men while examining the facts of their accomplishments without being impressed by the tremendous potentialities that underlie their efforts.

Almost the first discovery is that the organized farmers have ideals beyond material advantage and that these ideals are national in scope, therefore involving responsibilities. Undeterred by these, the farmers are eager to push on to further achievements. Their hope for these ideals lies in the success of their business undertakings and it is because that success is the spinal column of the whole movement that it occupies such a prominent place in this historical outline.

Not all the Grain Growers are men of vision, it must be admitted. Many have joined the movement for what they can get out of it. In all great aggregations of human beings it is quite possible to discover the full gamut of human failings. But loose threads sticking to a piece of cloth are no part of its warp and woof. It is the thinking Grain Grower who must be reckoned with and he is in the majority; the others are being educated.

If there is doubt as to the sincerity of the organized farmers, why did their pioneer business agency spend its substance in educational directions instead of solely along the straight commercial lines of the concerns with which it was in competition? The very mould into which it poured its energies shaped special difficulties, generated special antagonisms and every possible obstruction to its progress. Its cash grants to the Associations in the West, to the official organ of the movement, even to the Ontario farmers, run over the hundred-thousand-dollar mark.

Or, take the case of the Grain Growers at Virden, Manitoba, who proposed to bring into the district a large shipment of binder twine to supply their members. When the local merchant who had been handling this necessity learned of the plan he raised his voice, thus:

"If you fellows are going to do that then I go out of binder twine this season. I won't handle a pound of it."

"Not even to supply the farmers who don't belong to our Association?"

"That's what I said. You're going to make a convenience of me when you rob me of all my cash business. The only business I could do would be with farmers who wanted credit."

Did the Grain Growers say: "That's their lookout, then. Let them join us or go twineless"? No. They decided to bring in their co-operative shipment as planned, but to allow the merchant to handle it on commission in order to prevent any injustice to the other farmers.

Incidents like that can be recorded from all over the country. It does not take very many of them to compel the honest conviction that equity of citizenship for all the people in every walk of life means more to these farmers than a high-sounding shibboleth. That being so, it becomes difficult to accept the slur of utter selfishness—the idea that the farmers are auto-intoxicated, a pig-headed lot who cause trouble for nothing. It is very hard to believe that Everybody Else is good and kind and sincere and true, affectionate one to another with brotherly love, not slothful in business; for one knows that the best of us need the prayers of our mothers!

When these Grain Growers started out they did not know very much about what was going on. They had their suspicions; but that was all. To-day they know. Their business activities have taught them many things while providing the resources for the fight that is shaping unless the whole monopolistic system lets go its stranglehold.

Yes, the farmers do talk about freedom in buying and selling; also about tariff reform. They point out that there are criminal laws to jail bankers who dared to charge from twenty-five per cent. to forty-two per cent. for the use of money; that food and clothing and the necessaries of life are the same as money and that high tariff protection which fosters combines and monopolies is official discrimination against the many in favor of the few; that there are other and more just forms of taxation and that all old systems of patronage and campaign funds have got to go if the grave problems of these grave times are to be met successfully.

It is no old-time "Hayseed" who is discussing these things. It is a New Farmer altogether. The Farmers' Movement is no fancy of the moment either, but the product of Time itself. It is a condition which has developed in our rural life as the corolla of increased opportunities for education. The Farmer to-day is a different man to what he was ten years ago—indeed, five years ago.

It has taken fifteen years of bitter struggle for the Western farmers to win to their present position and now that they are far enough along their Trail to Better Things to command respect they are going to say what they think without fear or favor. They believe the principles for which they stand to be fundamental to national progress.

If there is to be any attempt to cram the old order of things down the people's throats; if, under cloak of all this present talk of winning the war, of new eras and of patriotism, profiteers should scheme and plan fresh campaigns—then will there be such a wrathful rising of the people as will sweep everything before it. In the forefront of that battle will stand the rugged legions of the organized farmers.

Make no miscalculation of their ability to fight. This year, 1918, will see them sawing their own lumber in their own saw-mills in British Columbia. If necessary, they can grind their own flour in their own flour mills, dig their own coal from their own mines, run their own packing-plants, provide their own fidelity and fire-insurance, finance their own undertakings. They grow the grain. They produce the new wealth from the soil. They are the men who create our greatest asset, everything else revolving upon the axis of Agriculture in Canada.

If, then, the farming population has learned to co-operate and stand solid; if in addition they have acquired the necessary capital to educate the masses and are prepared to spend it in advancing their ideals; if the working classes of the cities and the soldier citizens of Coming Days join their ranks— what chance will Special Privilege have against the public desire for Equal Rights?

Is it to be co-operation in all sincerity or class warfare? If the other great interests in our national life will meet the Farmer in a fair spirit, approaching our national problems in an honest attempt to co-operate in their solution for the common good, they will find the Farmer meeting them eagerly. They will find that these farmer leaders are reasonable men, broad-minded, square-principled and just—no less so because the class they represent is organized to stand up for its rights.

The situation is not hopeless. Most of these pages we have been turning are Back Pages. Old conditions and much of the bitterness which they generated have passed. The story of those old conditions has been told from the viewpoint of the Farmer in order that his attitude may be understood. But it must be remembered that the grain trade to-day is a very different proposition to what it was and that many of the men who have devoted their lives to it in the cities have played a big and honest part in its development. The Winnipeg Grain Exchange as an Exchange has done a great deal for Western Canada, a point that undoubtedly has been overlooked by many farmers. Gradually, however, the Farmer has learned that all is not evil in "Babylon"; for out of revolution has come evolution.[1]

The key to that better future which is desired so earnestly and wisely is Education. The problems of the day are commanding the mental focus of the nation. The Banks, the Railways, the Manufacturers are considering them. The Joint Committee of Commerce and Agriculture has great opportunities for removing much old-time hostility on both sides. And now that true co-operation of all classes has become a national duty, surely out of the testing must come better understanding and a greater future.

Just now, of course, there is only the War. It has brought the Canadian people to their feet. For the angry glare of the gun flashes has thrown in silhouette many fallacies, many foibles and rubbish heaps, and these must be swept out in preparation for the new nationhood which Canada is called upon to assume. With a third of the entire British Empire entrusted to her management and the hopeful gaze of homemakers the world over turning upon her Canada's responsibilities are great. But she will rise to her opportunities.

Just now there is only the War. The history of mankind has no previous record of such chaos, such a solemn time. Thrones toppling, maps changing, whole peoples dying of starvation and misery while the fate of Democracy is balanced on the issue. Men are slaying each other on land, in the air, on the water and below it while the forces of Destruction are gnawing holes in the World's resources with the rapacity of swarming rats. It is costing Great Britain alone over thirty-five million dollars every day—a million and a half every hour!

As for Canada—much figuring is being done by experts and others in attempts to estimate the total debt which the Canadian people will have to carry after the war. But the people themselves are too far immersed in war efforts to pause for futile reckonings. There will be time enough for that when the war is won, and won it shall be, no matter what the cost. It requires no great perspicacity to realize that our total national debt will be a sum which rolls so easily on its ciphers that it eludes the grasp of the average mind. It is going to cost a lot even to keep the wheels greased at five and one-half per cent. from year to year. Everybody knows it. *Win the War!*

When the lamp went out and the old world we had known blew up—away back in 1914—we spagged about anxiously, calling to each other: "Business as Usual!" Since then factory production has gone up fifty per cent.; export trade a hundred; profits on capital all the way up to the billion-and-a-quarter mark. We have got so used to things in four years that there is danger of forgetting that War has driven a sap beneath these ironical gifts of Mars and it is full time Business looked around for a place to light and got ready to dig itself in.

Mobilization, co-operation of every interest, the full grapple of every individual—national effort, in short—these the State demands. The coverlet has been thrown back upon the realization that the State has claims upon each citizen which transcend his individual fortunes—that individual prosperity, in fact, is entirely dependent upon the prosperity of the national whole.

Not all by himself can the Man Behind The Gun win a war like this. At his heels must stand the munition workers, the Man Back of The Desk, the people themselves, each guarding against waste and each contributing his or her part, great or small, for that national economy which alone can hope to sustain the terrific pace that victory demands. Finally, out in the great open spaces, faithful and unassuming and backing his country to the limit, must plod the Man Behind The Plow, working silently and steadily from dawn till dark to enlist and re-enlist the horizoned acres.

Canada has reason for pride in her farmers. No class is more loyal to British traditions. No class is more determined to win this war. Thousands of their sons are at the front. Many a lonely mother has stood on a prairie knoll, straining her eyes for the last glimpse of the buggy and bravely waving "God-speed." In many a windswept prairie farm home reigns the sad pride of sacrifice.

Out of the sanctifying fires is arising a national tendency to new viewpoints. The hope of Canada lies in a more active participation in affairs by the Average Citizen. In opposition to an awakened national interest what chance is there going to be for the silent partnerships of "invisible government"? 'Twill be a sorry partizan who allows his thoughts at this crisis to patter away at that old practice line, so full of past mistakes: "Now is the time for all good men to come to the aid of the Party."

Win-the-War unity is the leaven at work in Canada to-day and regeneration is coming.

What does it matter except that our country's leaders shall rise to their opportunities for true statesmanship with a deep sense of their responsibilities to the millions who turn to them for guidance in this time of national stress? What does it matter except that the people shall grant to their leaders their sympathy and co-operation in the cares of crisis?

As this book goes to the publisher Union Government in Canada has become a fact. Not since Confederation has such a thing happened in this country. The vampire methods with which our political system has been cursed have been thrown under foot and thinking Canadians everywhere have drawn a breath of relief. The energies which have been wasted in jockeying for party position are now concentrating upon effective unity of action. Let us hope so indeed. There must be no want of confidence in the cheers which echo from Canadian trenches.

For over there where Canada's first line of defence runs from the North Sea through Belgium into France your boy, Mr. Business Man, and your boy, Mr. Farmer, stand shoulder to shoulder. Think you that in the crucible which bares the very souls of men those boys have any thought of class criticism or of selfish grabbings? In those trenches you will find more practical Christianity, more unselfishness, more true brother-hood than can be realized at this distance. The spirit of sacrifice, the help-one-another idea, the equal share and charity of thought—these revitalizing principles will be brought back by our khaki citizens when they march home from victory. It is past belief that there should be anything but complete unity of purpose as they look back for their country's supports.

A coat of arms on the red field of a British flag, a maple leaf on khaki cap or collar-band, a single name on every shoulder-strap—CANADA. All the nations of the earth salute that name. For it is emblazoned on the shell-churned fields of Ypres where, sweltering and bleeding, Canada "saved the day" for all humanity. It is inscribed for all time to come on the Somme—on Vimy Ridge—on the difficult slopes of Passchendaele.

Just now, only the War.

But when in the Years To Be we find ourselves in some far land or in some international circle which Chance, mayhap, has thrown together; when the talk turns upon the Great War and the wonderful victory of Civilization; when we are questioned as to who and what we are and we reply simply: "Gentlemen, I am a Canadian"—

Then may the light of pride in our eyes be undimmed by any sense of shame for duty shunned. May it be that out of it all has arisen a higher conception of individual and national life. So that in place of deep furrows of dissension there will be the level seed-bed of greater unity and justice among men.

THE END

[1] Abnormal conditions in the grain trade at present, due to the war, have led to government control of the crop by means of a Board of Grain Supervisors, aside altogether from the permanent Board of Grain Commissioners. This government commission has very wide powers, superseding the Grain Act for the time being, and can fix the price at which grain stored in any elevator may be purchased, ascertain available supplies, fix conditions of removal from storage and determine the destination of grain, receive purchase offers and fix sale prices, take possession of grain in elevators and sell it, provide transportation, etc.

The Board of Grain Supervisors consists of two representatives of the organized farmers—Hon. T. A. Crerar, Minister of Agriculture, and H. W. Wood, President of United Farmers of Alberta; one representative of unorganised farmers—S. K. Rathwell; three representatives of the Winnipeg Grain Exchange—J. C. Gage, W. E. Bawlf and Dr. Magill (Chairman); a representative of the British Food Commission—Jas. Stewart; two representatives of Labor—Controller Ainey (Montreal) and W. B. Best, of Locomotive Firemen; W. A. Matheson, of Lake of the Woods Milling Company, and Lionel H. Clarke, head of the Canada Malting Company and a member of the Toronto Harbor Commission. Dr. Robert Magill, the Chairman, is Secretary of the Winnipeg Grain Exchange and was formerly Chief Commissioner of the permanent Board of Grain Commissioners.

APPENDIX

FIRST OFFICERS, DIRECTORS, COMMITTEES, ETC., OF THE FARMERS' MOVEMENT IN WESTERN CANADA, ETC.

1. *Territorial* (Saskatchewan) *Grain Growers' Association—1902.*

President, W. R. Motherwell (Abernethy); Secretary, John Millar (Indian Head). Among those who acted on the first Board of Directors were: Messrs. Walter Govan and M. M. Warden (Indian Head); John Gillespie, Elmer Shaw and Peter Dayman (Abernethy); Matthew Snow (Wolseley).

2. *Virden* (Manitoba) *Grain Growers' Association—1903.*

President, J. W. Scallion; Vice-president, George Carefoot; Secretary-Treasurer, H. W. Dayton; Directors: J. A. Blakeman, Isaac Bennett, Peter McDonald and C. E. Ivens.

3. *Manitoba Grain Growers' Association—1903.*

President, J. W. Scallion (Virden); Vice-President, R. C. Henders (Culross); Secretary-Treasurer, R. McKenzie (Brandon); Directors: Donald McEwan, Brandon; William Ryan (Boissevain), W. A. Robinson (Elva), D. W. McCuaig

(Portage la Prairie), John Wilson (Lenore), and H. A. Fraser, Hamiota.

4. *Committee to Investigate Possibilities of Farmers Trading in Grain—1905.*

The first step towards co-operative trading in grain by the farmers of Western Canada was a scheme, fathered by E. A. Partridge, of Sintaluta, Sask., the first official action being taken by the Manitoba Grain Growers' Association at their annual convention in 1905, when the following committee was ordered to investigate and report:

Chairman, E. A. Partridge (Sintaluta, Sask.); J. A. Taylor (Cartwright, Man.); A. S. Barton (Boissevain, Man.).

5. *Local Committee to Organise Meeting of Sintaluta Farmers—1906.*

The following committee of Sintaluta farmers made arrangements for a meeting of the farmers in the Sintaluta district to discuss co-operative trading in grain and to pledge support of the trading company proposed by E. A. Partridge:

E. A. Partridge, Al Quigley, Dave Railton, W. J. Bonner, T. McLeod, James Ewart.

6. *Preliminary Organisation Committee of Sintaluta Farmers—1906.*

E. A. Partridge (Chairman), A. J. Quigley (Secretary), William Hall (Treasurer), James Halford, James Ewart, D. Railton, Sr., J. O. Partridge, William J. Bonner, Thomas S. McLeod, W. Malhiot, H. O. Partridge, G. K. Grass, Harold Bird, H. T. Smith, George Hill—all of Sintaluta, Sask.

Subsequently this committee was enlarged to include a number of Manitoba canvassers.

7. Provisional Officers of Grain Growers' Grain Company— 1906.

Provisional organization of the Western farmers' pioneer trading company finally took place at Winnipeg, July 26th, 1906, when the following officers were chosen:

President, E. A. Partridge; Vice-President, John Kennedy; Secretary-Treasurer, John Spencer; Directors: W. A. Robinson (Elva, Man.), and Francis Graham (Melita, Man.).

At a general meeting of the shareholders these same officers were elected subsequently and the directorate increased by two—Robert Cruise (Dauphin) and T. W. Knowles (Emerson).

8. Sintaluta (Sask.) *Farmers Who Pledged Personal Securities—1906.*

Finding themselves $1,500 short of the necessary $2,500 for the purchase of a seat on the Winnipeg Grain Exchange, the young trading company of farmers had recourse to personal securities in order to finance their start in business. The friends to whom E. A. Partridge appealed and who immediately gave the bank their personal notes were the following Sintaluta men:

Dave Railton, Al Quigley, Tom McLeod, Jim Ewart, William E. Hall.

9. Inter-Provincial Council of Grain Growers' and Farmers' Associations—1907.

It was under this name that the executive officers of the various farmers' organizations in the three Prairie Provinces first came together to discuss problems affecting the Movement as a whole. The first officers of the Inter-Provincial Council were:

President, E. N. Hopkins (Moose Jaw, Sask.); Secretary, M. D. Geddes (Calgary, Alberta).

10. *United Farmers of Alberta—1909.*

Until January 14th, 1909, the farmers of Alberta had two provincial organizations—the "Canadian Society of Equity" and the "Alberta Farmers' Association." On this date amalgamation took place at Edmonton under the name, "United Farmers of Alberta" with officers and directors as follows:

President, James Bower (Red Deer); Vice-President, Rice Sheppard (Strathcona); Secretary, Edward J. Fream (Calgary); Directors: G. A. Dixon (Fishburn), A. Von Mielecki (Calgary), George McDonald (Olds), George Long (Edmonton), Thomas Balaam (Vegreville), L. H. Jelliffe (Spring Coulee), E. Carswell (Penhold), H. Jamieson (Red Deer).

11. *Canadian Council of Agriculture—1910.*

The name of the Inter-Provincial Council (Par. 9) was changed to the "Canadian Council of Agriculture" in 1909 when relations were established with The Grange, the early organization of Ontario farmers. The first officers of the new inter-provincial body were:

President, D. W. McCuaig (Portage la Prairie, Man.); Vice-president, James Bower (Red Deer, Alberta); Secretary, E. C.

Drury (Barrie, Ont.).

12. *Saskatchewan Co-Operative Elevator Company—1911.*

Provisional Officers: President, J. A. Maharg (Moose Jaw); Vice-president, F. W. Green (Moose Jaw); Secretary-Treasurer, Charles A. Dunning (Beaverdale); Directors: A. G. Hawkes (Percival), James Robinson (Walpole), Dr. T. Hill (Kinley).

Upon early withdrawal of F. W. Green for personal reasons, George Langley (Maymont) was called by the Board in an advisory capacity.

First Election: President, J. A. Maharg (Moose Jaw); Vice-President, George Langley (Maymont); Secretary-Treasurer, Charles A. Dunning (Beaverdale); Directors: James Robinson (Walpole), W. C. Sutherland (Saskatoon), N. E. Baumunk (Dundurn), A. G. Hawkes (Percival), J. E. Paynter (Tantallon), Dr. E. J. Barrick.

13. *Alberta Farmers' Co-Operative Elevator Company— 1913.*

Provisional Officers: President, W. J. Tregillus (Calgary); Vice-President, E. Carswell (Red Deer); Secretary-Treasurer, E. J. Fream (Calgary); Directors: Joseph Quinsey (Noble), William S. Henry (Bow Island), Rice Sheppard (Edmonton), P. P. Woodbridge (Calgary).

First Election: President, W. J. Tregillus; Vice-president, J. Quinsey (Noble); Secretary-Treasurer, E. J. Fream (Calgary); Directors: E. Carswell (Red Deer), Rice Sheppard (Edmonton), P. S. Austin (Ranfurly), J. G. McKay (Provost), R. A. Parker (Winnifred), C. Rice-Jones (Veteran).

14. *United Farmers of Ontario—1914.*

Organisation Committee—1913: E. C. Drury (Barrie), J. J. Morrison (Arthur), Henry Glendinning (Manilla), Elmer Lick (Oshawa), H. B. Cowan (Peterboro), W. C. Good (Paris), Col. J. Z. Frazer (Burford).

First Election of Officers—1914: President, E. C. Drury (Barrie); Secretary-Treasurer, J. J. Morrison (Arthur).

15. *United Farmers' Co-Operative Company, Limited—1914.*

President, W. C. Good (Paris); Secretary-Treasurer, J. J. Morrison (Arthur); Executive: Anson Groh (Preston), C. W. Gurney (Paris), Col. J. Z. Fraser (Burford), E. C. Drury (Barrie).

16. *United Farmers of British Columbia—1917.*

Provisional Committee (Vancouver Island Farmers' Union)—*1916*: Chairman, R. M. Palmer (Cowichan Bay); Secretary-Treasurer, W. Paterson (Duncan); H. G. Helgesen (Metchosin), G. A. Cheeke (Shawnigan Lake), A. E. Brooke Wilkinson (Cobble Hill), E. H. Forrest (Hillbank), F. J. Bishop (Cowichan Station), G. H. Hadwen (Comiaken), C. G. Palmer, C.I.E. (Quamichan), F. Maris Hale (Deerholme), A. A. Mutter (Somenos), L. F. Solly (Westholme), R. U. Hurford (Courtenay), A. C. Aiken (Duncan).

First Election (United Farmers of British Columbia)—*1917*: President, C. G. Palmer (Quamichan); Vice-Presidents: J. W. Berry (Langley), R. A. Copeland (Kelowna), P. H. Moore (Saanich); Secretary, H. J. Ruscombe Poole (Duncan); Directors: J. Johnson (Nelson), R. U. Hurford (Comox), L. Dilworth (Kelowna), R. H. Helmer (Summerland), W. E.

Smith (Revelstoke), W. Paterson (Koksiloh).

17. *United Grain Growers, Limited—1917.*

By Act of Dominion Parliament, June, 1917, the necessary changes in the charter of the Grain Growers' Grain Company, Limited, were granted to enable amalgamation with the Alberta Farmers' Co-Operative Elevator Company under the name, "United Grain Growers, Limited"; authorized capital, $5,000,000. The first election of officers was as follows:

President, T. A. Crerar; 1st Vice-president, C. Rice-Jones (Veteran, Alta.); 2nd Vice-president, John Kennedy; Secretary, E. J. Fream (Calgary, Alta.); Directors: C. F. Brown (Calgary), R. A. Parker (Winnifred, Alta.), J. J. McLellan (Purple Springs, Alta.), P. S. Austin (Banfurly, Alta.), H. C. Wingate (Cayley, Alta.), Roderick McKenzie (Brandon, Man.), F. J. Collyer (Welwyn, Sask.), John Morrison (Yellow Grass, Sask.), J. F. Reid (Orcadia, Sask.).

18. At the meeting of the Canadian Council of Agriculture in Winnipeg on July 5th, 1918, Norman P. Lambert was appointed Secretary-Treasurer to succeed Roderick McKenzie, who now occupies the position of Vice-president.

19. R. A. Bonnar, K.C. (Bonnar, Trueman, Hollands & Robinson), has been solicitor and counsel for the Grain Growers since 1906 and has been identified closely with them on many dramatic occasions.

Choose from Thousands of 1stWorldLibrary Classics By

A. M. Barnard
Ada Leverson
Adolphus William Ward
Aesop
Agatha Christie
Alexander Aaronsohn
Alexander Kielland
Alexandre Dumas
Alfred Gatty
Alfred Ollivant
Alice Duer Miller
Alice Turner Curtis
Alice Dunbar
Allen Chapman
Alleyne Ireland
Ambrose Bierce
Amelia E. Barr
Amory H. Bradford
Andrew Lang
Andrew McFarland Davis
Andy Adams
Angela Brazil
Anna Alice Chapin
Anna Sewell
Annie Besant
Annie Hamilton Donnell
Annie Payson Call
Annie Roe Carr
Annonaymous
Anton Chekhov
Archibald Lee Fletcher
Arnold Bennett
Arthur C. Benson
Arthur Conan Doyle
Arthur M. Winfield
Arthur Ransome
Arthur Schnitzler
Arthur Train
Atticus
B.H. Baden-Powell
B. M. Bower
B. C. Chatterjee
Baroness Emmuska Orczy
Baroness Orczy
Basil King
Bayard Taylor
Ben Macomber
Bertha Muzzy Bower
Bjornstjerne Bjornson

Booth Tarkington
Boyd Cable
Bram Stoker
C. Collodi
C. E. Orr
C. M. Ingleby
Carolyn Wells
Catherine Parr Traill
Charles A. Eastman
Charles Amory Beach
Charles Dickens
Charles Dudley Warner
Charles Farrar Browne
Charles Ives
Charles Kingsley
Charles Klein
Charles Hanson Towne
Charles Lathrop Pack
Charles Romyn Dake
Charles Whibley
Charles Willing Beale
Charlotte M. Braeme
Charlotte M. Yonge
Charlotte Perkins Stetson
Clair W. Hayes
Clarence Day Jr.
Clarence E. Mulford
Clemence Housman
Confucius
Coningsby Dawson
Cornelis DeWitt Wilcox
Cyril Burleigh
D. H. Lawrence
Daniel Defoe
David Garnett
Dinah Craik
Don Carlos Janes
Donald Keyhoe
Dorothy Kilner
Dougan Clark
Douglas Fairbanks
E. Nesbit
E. P. Roe
E. Phillips Oppenheim
E. S. Brooks
Earl Barnes
Edgar Rice Burroughs
Edith Van Dyne
Edith Wharton

Edward Everett Hale
Edward J. O'Biren
Edward S. Ellis
Edwin L. Arnold
Eleanor Atkins
Eleanor Hallowell Abbott
Eliot Gregory
Elizabeth Gaskell
Elizabeth McCracken
Elizabeth Von Arnim
Ellem Key
Emerson Hough
Emilie F. Carlen
Emily Bronte
Emily Dickinson
Enid Bagnold
Enilor Macartney Lane
Erasmus W. Jones
Ernie Howard Pie
Ethel May Dell
Ethel Turner
Ethel Watts Mumford
Eugene Sue
Eugenie Foa
Eugene Wood
Eustace Hale Ball
Evelyn Everett-green
Everard Cotes
F. H. Cheley
F. J. Cross
F. Marion Crawford
Fannie E. Newberry
Federick Austin Ogg
Ferdinand Ossendowski
Fergus Hume
Florence A. Kilpatrick
Fremont B. Deering
Francis Bacon
Francis Darwin
Frances Hodgson Burnett
Frances Parkinson Keyes
Frank Gee Patchin
Frank Harris
Frank Jewett Mather
Frank L. Packard
Frank V. Webster
Frederic Stewart Isham
Frederick Trevor Hill
Frederick Winslow Taylor

Friedrich Kerst
Friedrich Nietzsche
Fyodor Dostoyevsky
G.A. Henty
G.K. Chesterton
Gabrielle E. Jackson
Garrett P. Serviss
Gaston Leroux
George A. Warren
George Ade
Geroge Bernard Shaw
George Cary Eggleston
George Durston
George Ebers
George Eliot
George Gissing
George MacDonald
George Meredith
George Orwell
George Sylvester Viereck
George Tucker
George W. Cable
George Wharton James
Gertrude Atherton
Gordon Casserly
Grace E. King
Grace Gallatin
Grace Greenwood
Grant Allen
Guillermo A. Sherwell
Gulielma Zollinger
Gustav Flaubert
H. A. Cody
H. B. Irving
H.C. Bailey
H. G. Wells
H. H. Munro
H. Irving Hancock
H. R. Naylor
H. Rider Haggard
H. W. C. Davis
Haldeman Julius
Hall Caine
Hamilton Wright Mabie
Hans Christian Andersen
Harold Avery
Harold McGrath
Harriet Beecher Stowe
Harry Castlemon
Harry Coghill
Harry Houidini

Hayden Carruth
Helent Hunt Jackson
Helen Nicolay
Hendrik Conscience
Hendy David Thoreau
Henri Barbusse
Henrik Ibsen
Henry Adams
Henry Ford
Henry Frost
Henry James
Henry Jones Ford
Henry Seton Merriman
Henry W Longfellow
Herbert A. Giles
Herbert Carter
Herbert N. Casson
Herman Hesse
Hildegard G. Frey
Homer
Honore De Balzac
Horace B. Day
Horace Walpole
Horatio Alger Jr.
Howard Pyle
Howard R. Garis
Hugh Lofting
Hugh Walpole
Humphry Ward
Ian Maclaren
Inez Haynes Gillmore
Irving Bacheller
Isabel Cecilia Williams
Isabel Hornibrook
Israel Abrahams
Ivan Turgenev
J.G.Austin
J. Henri Fabre
J. M. Barrie
J. M. Walsh
J. Macdonald Oxley
J. R. Miller
J. S. Fletcher
J. S. Knowles
J. Storer Clouston
J. W. Duffield
Jack London
Jacob Abbott
James Allen
James Andrews
James Baldwin

James Branch Cabell
James DeMille
James Joyce
James Lane Allen
James Lane Allen
James Oliver Curwood
James Oppenheim
James Otis
James R. Driscoll
Jane Abbott
Jane Austen
Jane L. Stewart
Janet Aldridge
Jens Peter Jacobsen
Jerome K. Jerome
Jessie Graham Flower
John Buchan
John Burroughs
John Cournos
John F. Kennedy
John Gay
John Glasworthy
John Habberton
John Joy Bell
John Kendrick Bangs
John Milton
John Philip Sousa
John Taintor Foote
Jonas Lauritz Idemil Lie
Jonathan Swift
Joseph A. Altsheler
Joseph Carey
Joseph Conrad
Joseph E. Badger Jr
Joseph Hergesheimer
Joseph Jacobs
Jules Vernes
Julian Hawthrone
Julie A Lippmann
Justin Huntly McCarthy
Kakuzo Okakura
Karle Wilson Baker
Kate Chopin
Kenneth Grahame
Kenneth McGaffey
Kate Langley Bosher
Kate Langley Bosher
Katherine Cecil Thurston
Katherine Stokes
L. A. Abbot
L. T. Meade

L. Frank Baum
Latta Griswold
Laura Dent Crane
Laura Lee Hope
Laurence Housman
Lawrence Beasley
Leo Tolstoy
Leonid Andreyev
Lewis Carroll
Lewis Sperry Chafer
Lilian Bell
Lloyd Osbourne
Louis Hughes
Louis Joseph Vance
Louis Tracy
Louisa May Alcott
Lucy Fitch Perkins
Lucy Maud Montgomery
Luther Benson
Lydia Miller Middleton
Lyndon Orr
M. Corvus
M. H. Adams
Margaret E. Sangster
Margret Howth
Margaret Vandercook
Margaret W. Hungerford
Margret Penrose
Maria Edgeworth
Maria Thompson Daviess
Mariano Azuela
Marion Polk Angellotti
Mark Overton
Mark Twain
Mary Austin
Mary Catherine Crowley
Mary Cole
Mary Hastings Bradley
Mary Roberts Rinehart
Mary Rowlandson
M. Wollstonecraft Shelley
Maud Lindsay
Max Beerbohm
Myra Kelly
Nathaniel Hawthrone
Nicolo Machiavelli
O. F. Walton
Oscar Wilde

Owen Johnson
P.G. Wodehouse
Paul and Mabel Thorne
Paul G. Tomlinson
Paul Severing
Percy Brebner
Percy Keese Fitzhugh
Peter B. Kyne
Plato
Quincy Allen
R. Derby Holmes
R. L. Stevenson
R. S. Ball
Rabindranath Tagore
Rahul Alvares
Ralph Bonehill
Ralph Henry Barbour
Ralph Victor
Ralph Waldo Emmerson
Rene Descartes
Ray Cummings
Rex Beach
Rex E. Beach
Richard Harding Davis
Richard Jefferies
Richard Le Gallienne
Robert Barr
Robert Frost
Robert Gordon Anderson
Robert L. Drake
Robert Lansing
Robert Lynd
Robert Michael Ballantyne
Robert W. Chambers
Rosa Nouchette Carey
Rudyard Kipling
Saint Augustine
Samuel B. Allison
Samuel Hopkins Adams
Sarah Bernhardt
Sarah C. Hallowell
Selma Lagerlof
Sherwood Anderson
Sigmund Freud
Standish O'Grady
Stanley Weyman
Stella Benson
Stella M. Francis

Stephen Crane
Stewart Edward White
Stijn Streuvels
Swami Abhedananda
Swami Parmananda
T. S. Ackland
T. S. Arthur
The Princess Der Ling
Thomas A. Janvier
Thomas A Kempis
Thomas Anderton
Thomas Bailey Aldrich
Thomas Bulfinch
Thomas De Quincey
Thomas Dixon
Thomas H. Huxley
Thomas Hardy
Thomas More
Thornton W. Burgess
U. S. Grant
Upton Sinclair
Valentine Williams
Various Authors
Vaughan Kester
Victor Appleton
Victor G. Durham
Victoria Cross
Virginia Woolf
Wadsworth Camp
Walter Camp
Walter Scott
Washington Irving
Wilbur Lawton
Wilkie Collins
Willa Cather
Willard F. Baker
William Dean Howells
William le Queux
W. Makepeace Thackeray
William W. Walter
William Shakespeare
Winston Churchill
Yei Theodora Ozaki
Yogi Ramacharaka
Young E. Allison
Zane Grey